SNOWDONIA

160 pages of

BEST WOODLAND WALKS

Editor: Thomas Sion Jones

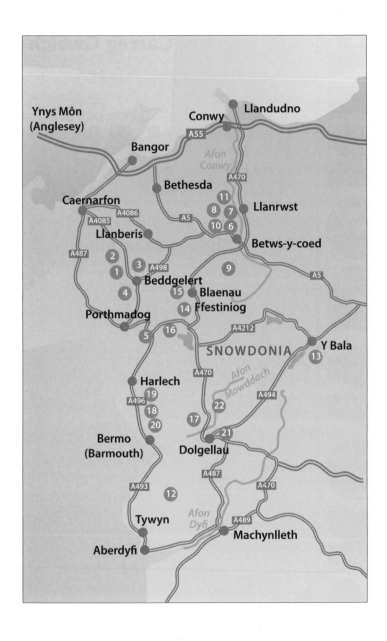

Contents

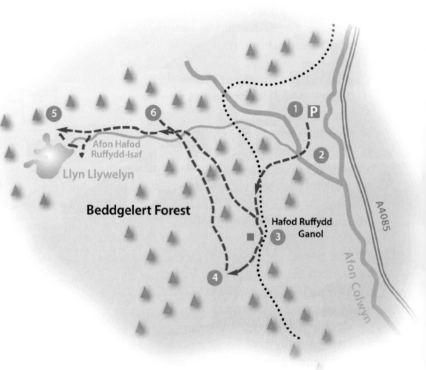

Walk 1
Beddgelert Forest

Walk details

Approx distance: *3 miles/5 kilometres*

Approx time: *1½ hours*

O.S. Maps: *1:50 000 Landranger Sheet 115*
1:25 000 Explorer OL 17

Start: *Beddgelert Forest car park*
Grid Ref. SH 574502

Access: *The car park is off the A4085, north of Beddgelert. Take a track on the left signposted Beddgelert Forest, half a mile north of the forest camp site. After 600m turn right into the car park.*

Parking: *Beddgelert Forest car park, free of charge.*

Please note: *Rough stony track at point 6.*

Going: *This walk follows forest tracks, some of them uphill, to a lovely lake in a woodland setting.*

Beddgelert Forest is a magnificent, coniferous woodland on the eastern slopes of mountains in the Moel Hebog range. The trees were first planted in 1926 and many have been felled, opening up views of Snowdonia's mountains. This walk takes you to a beautiful, small lake surrounded by trees below Moel Lefn. According to legend, the hollow holding the lake was made by a giant who jumped from a rock whilst taking part in a jumping contest with another giant. It is a fine spot for a picnic.

Walk directions: (-) **denotes Point of Interest**
1. From the car park, walk down to the lower track towards the entrance, opposite the information board walk down a narrow path. It goes downhill beside overhead wires and emerges on a track.

2.   Turn right to cross an old stone bridge called Pont Rhyd Ceffylau and ignore a track on the left. Follow the track as it crosses the Welsh Highland Railway line and curves to the left. Ignore path 57 on the right and pass a drive to a house and ignore two tracks on the right. Ignore a path and gate on right. Continue along the main track beside a right-hand wall.

3.   At the next track on the right, signed Hafod Ruffydd Uchaf, go right along it. When the track bends right, go left on a lesser track and pass around a barrier. Follow it uphill to a broad forest track.

4.   Turn right and there will soon be fine views of Snowdonia. Ignore a track on the left and walk downhill to cross a bridge. Reach a track crossroads and turn left uphill on a rough track and keep ahead at a track junction. After about another 200 metres, you will see Llyn Llywelyn on your left.

5. Turn left on a path. There are picnic tables beside

The Royal Goat Hotel, near the car park in Beddgelert

the lake. When you are ready to leave, follow the path over a small bridge to a forest track. Turn left to the track crossroads and turn right to retrace your steps via a small gate to the crossroads lower down.

6. Cross directly over and walk downhill on a rough track. A stream is heard rumbling down on your right. Stay on the track to emerge on a broad forest track, where you turn left to retrace your steps over the railway line and bridge to the start of your walk.

Originally published in
Short Family Walks in Snowdonia

by Dorothy Hamilton

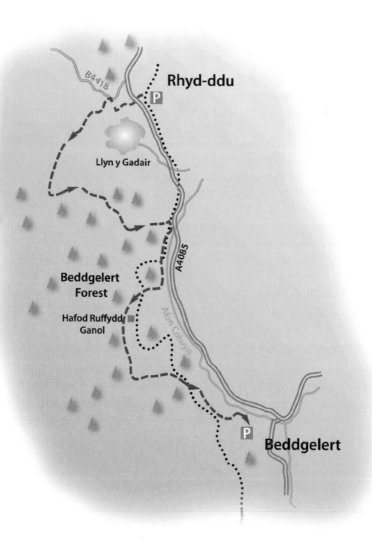

Walk 2
Nant Colwyn Valley
(Rhyd-ddu to Beddgelert)

Walk details

Approx distance: *5 miles/8 kilometres*

Approx time: *3 hours*

O.S. Maps: *1:50 000 Landranger Sheet 115*
1:25 000 Explorer OL 17 S

Start: *Either from Beddgelert car park (Grid Ref. SH 588 481) or Rhyd-ddu car park (Grid Ref. SH 5715270)*

Access: *Off the A4086 (Caernarfon/Beddgelert)*

Parking: *Pay and display car parks in Beddgelert or Rhyd-ddu (close to halt/station).*

Going: *Good forestry roads, can be wet at start and close to finish.*

This walk can be accomplished when the weather does not allow you to venture onto the higher tops. It can also be used by mountain bikers, but a little care is required at the start and finish of the route. The walk starts from the station car park at Rhyd-ddu. This station was once the terminus of the North Wales Narrow Gauge Railway's extension to the Moel Tryfan undertaking. This extension line from the main route serviced both the Glanrafon and Ffridd quarries.

In spite of the stations locality, situated on an extremely exposed position at an altitude of 626ft (191 meters) and close to the lines summit at Pitts Head at

Llyn y Gadair with Y Garn looming above the lake

647ft (197 meters), the station's original buildings were considerably larger than other stations on the line. The main buildings were constructed of brick and stone and there was a wooden refreshment hut for those passengers that were either waiting for the passenger service or a connection to Beddgelert by Charabanc. Nothing now remains of these buildings as the car park and toilet block are now located on the original site of the station.

The large house opposite the station was actually built as a hotel but unfortunately it was refused a license. Consequently, since then it has always been a private residence. The station has had a very chequered history. It was opened in May 1881 operating a passenger service, which continued up until part way through the hostilities of the First World War on 31st October 1916. The station was reopened on 31st July 1922, with the

Nant Colwyn, looking upriver towards Rhyd-ddu

extension of the track down to Beddgelert opening on the 1st June 1923. This allowed a connection to a passenger service, which continued through to Porthmadog. Passenger services were again to cease on the 26th June 1937 due to the closure of quarries within the locality. This led to the final closure of the line even for freight on 19th June 1937.

Hafod Ruffydd Isaf

The NWNGR must have thought there was a silver lining to all their efforts when, in spite of financial difficulties in 1875, C.E. Spooner Engineer to both the Ffestiniog Railway and the NWNGR proposed a rack railway be constructed to the summit of Snowdon. This would have led to an increase in the tourist trade in the Beddgelert area. Unfortunately for him, further financial problems caused the scheme to be dropped. It was fortunate for Llanberis because in 1893 a large deputation visited Assherton Smith, the local landowner and squire for Llanberis. He had been approached previously to ask if he would allow a railway to be built across his land to the summit of Snowdon. This time he agreed to the plan and as a consequence attracted tourism away from Beddgelert and into Llanberis.

The campsite in Beddgelert Forest

The walk which roughly follows the course of Nant Colwyn continues into the Beddgelert forest and along the many forestry tracks. The current forest was first planted by the Forestry Commission in 1926. Forestry plantations were in existence prior to this date as information indicates that wood from the forest was utilised in the construction of the Porthmadog,

Beddgelert and South Snowdon Railway. Again during World War 1 timber was transported, mostly horse drawn, from Cwm Ddu up to Rhyd-ddu and from Ty'n y Coed down to a point on the Beddgelert main road close to the Royal Goat Hotel.

The Walk: Depart the Station car park and cross the main road, to pass through a new entrance to Lôn Gwyrfai. The dry gravel path now crosses a boggy area, crossing a footbridge and bear left up to road. Through lane gate and immediately L to pass through metal gate and along grassy path. Through gate and continue to stile, over this and up to a prominent boulder with a white painted arrow.

1. At boulder go ½ L (boulder is junction with path to Y Garn) through gate and cross a stream. Continue on to cross a second stream. Pass through a gate into the forest, soon passing through a wall gap and crossing a forestry road. Pass between boulders and down to stream, now up onto bridge and L.

2. Follow forestry road and at first junction go R and at next junction (T junction) go L towards main road. Cross railway track and immediately go R down forestry road to pass parking area and wooden chalet on R.

3. At large property on L "Hafod Ruffydd Isaf" continue on for 50 meters then go R soon to cross a narrow road bridge over the river. Up to and over the railway track, soon passing "Hafod Ruffydd Canol". The road climbs to a T-junction, here go L. Pass lane to "Hafod Ruffydd

Uchaf" (Beics Beddgelert). At fork continue on. At left hand bend (railway just in sight) go ½ R along footpath to join forestry road. Now go L down to railway track (near campsite).

4. Just before railway track go R, forestry road runs parallel with railway track. Close to Campsite halt go ½ R up road passing barrier, continue on to sharp right hand bend. Here go L (footpath markers) to pass through a gate, cross a stream and through a second gate.

5. The path now follows the wall on the R and passes through a field gate to cross to footpath markers (Moel Hebog path). Go L down path to buildings. Pass through a gate and down the track crossing the railway track. Continue on down passing a farm on the L.

At the railway bridge (over the track), go R and soon L passing under the railway line and up to the Beddgelert station (or L down to car park).

Refreshments: In Rhyd-ddu just down from the car park/station is the Tŷ Mawr tea room, open all year and supplying home baked produce this is a welcome halt anytime of the year. Further down the road is the Cwellyn Arms, which serves pub grub.

Originally published in
Walks from the Welsh Highland Railway – Part 2

by Dave Salter and Dave Worrall

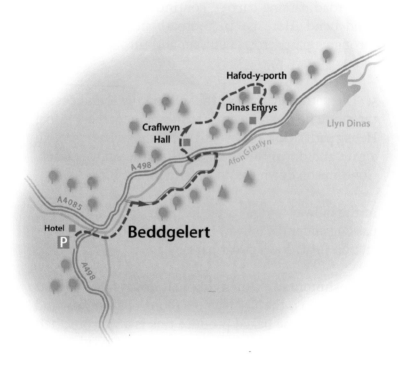

Walk 3
Vortigern's Fortress, Dinas Emrys

Walk details

Approx distance: *5 miles/8 kilometres*

Approx time: *3 hours, allowing time to explore*

O.S. Maps: *1:50 000 Landranger Sheet 115*
1:25 000 Explorer OL 17

Start: *Behind the Royal Goat Hotel*
Grid Ref. SH 588 481

Access: *From the A498, running through Beddgelert.*

Parking: *Beddgelert (behind Royal Goat Hotel) on A498.*
Car Park is pay and display.

Going: *Good riverside paths, then short section on main*
road (500 metres) before a rocky path to summit
which can be slippery when wet.

The walk out from Beddgelert is a very pleasant low level walk ideal for family exploration and will allow you to delve into Celtic Mythology and Arthurian legends of Dragons and Sorcery. The walk starts along a pleasant riverside footpath, which later passes close to the Sygun Copper mine. Unfortunately this mine is no longer extracting copper and has been developed into a thriving tourist centre. At Sygun the adventurous visitor can get kitted up with a miners lamp and follow the underground labyrinths followed by those miners of long ago. By entering the Victoria Level the budding miner can listen to a recorded commentary on the history of the mine which operated from 1825 until about 1901.

Care must be exercised when following the busy main road but all becomes tranquil when the drive past the lodge to Craflwyn Hall is reached. The hall's name "Craflwyn" is thought to derive from "Criafolen" (*mountain ash*) or "Craf" (*wild garlic*). Of course, these trees are in abundance in the area. The estate dates back to 1200AD, to the time when Prince Llywelyn the Great (Llywelyn ap Iorwerth of Gelert fame) donated land to the Cistercian Monks. The monks farmed this land as part of a Monastic Grange. Following Henry VIII's dissolution of the monasteries in 1536, the land was then farmed by Meredudd ab Ieuan, former steward of the monastic lands in the area. Probably following the marriage of the Steward's grand daughter Annes to Morys Jones, the estate passed into the ownership of the Jones family and by the early 1600's it was to become a gentry estate. The estate passed through the family from generation to generation carrying on the farming tradition. By 1873 it was to be run by Llywelyn Parry, whose initials and date appear on the gable of the lodge. He rebuilt the farmhouse and created a miniature estate, establishing woodland gardens and plantations. The family connection was severed after a period of 300 years when in 1895 the estate was sold. Unfortunately the property fell into disrepair due to the neglect of a succession of owners until it was obtained by the National Trust in 1994. They embarked on an extensive restoration programme. The Hall, restored to its former glory can now be used for conferences and weddings.

The walk passes over the slab bridge close to the falls

The path passes by Beddgelert bridge

The pedestrian bridge over Afon Glaslyn

of Afon y Cwm and then climbs into the mixed woodland surrounding Dinas Emrys and up to the fortress on the summit. Give yourself plenty of time to explore the remains of the 5th century hilltop fort and reflect on the mythology surrounding it. The story is left to us by the 9th century writer Nennius who tells us about the 5th century Brythonic king Vortigern who invited the Saxons into his kingdom to help defend it. Unfortunately for him the Saxons were to try and oust him from his Kingdom and with the advice of his wizards he fled to Gwynedd to establish his sanctuary. During the construction of his fortress his daily inspection revealed that the work the masons had completed the previous day had been completely destroyed. In desperate consultation with his wizards he was instructed that in order to break the spell the masons should slake the mortar with the blood of an illegitimate child. A search throughout Britain eventually found a child and he brought this child to the site in preparation for his sacrifice. On hearing of the reason for his pending sacrifice the child instructed Vortigern to enter a cave located in the base Dinas Emrys. Here, Vortigern was to discover the reason for the continual collapse of the walls. Two dragons, one white depicting the Saxons and the other red depicting the Celtic nations were fast asleep. However on rising from their slumbers, they commenced fighting, which caused the fortress walls to collapse. The child was in fact Myrddin Emrys (Ambrosius) also known as Merlin. His prophecy saw the red dragon of the Celts being successful in battle with the Saxons. Vortigern was to finally find sanctuary on the Llŷn Peninsula in Nant Gwrtheyrn where he was to spend the remainder of his life in isolation.

Unfortunately we must now retrace our steps unless the walker wishes to continue to the "Watkin Path" and then around Llyn Dinas. This will lengthen the walk considerably.

The Walk: Unfortunately areas of the National Trust estate at Craflwyn do not allow dogs to pass through.

Depart from Beddgelert station and walk down to the car park. In the car park go R to main road (A498). Go L along road to bridge. Cross the road and along lane, signposted Gelert's Grave and Toilets, with river on L and cross footbridge. Go L still with river on L crossing lane and through gate.

1. Continue along riverside path to a stile and lane. Cross stile and go R along lane to entrance of Sygun Mine. Here go L along access road to mine, crossing over bridge to main road.

2. Go L along main road for 500m to National Trust sign for Craflwyn (do not take drive up to Hall at first NT sign). Go R up the drive passing lodge on L to car park. Here it is worth crossing the car park to read the information boards, which explain about other walks available at Craflwyn. Return to drive then go L towards Hall.

3. At fork take L branch signed Stables/ Estate Office and pass between the rear of the hall and the converted stables and out through a gate into fields. Keep on along track to pass large enclosure on L. At end of track go L up to gate and continue on path passing through old

The Sygun Copper Mine

Dinas Emrys

wall gap. Here go R onto bridge and over stile (sign "Tir Gofal" Land being cared for). Keep going to nearby falls and cross slab bridge. Continue to wall corner and along with wall on R to stile.

4. Go R over stile and then L up grassy bank passing through mixed woodland to fence with stile. Cross fence and up to summit and fortress. Explore.

To return to Beddgelert retrace your outward steps

For those wishing to make a longer excursion, after visiting the summit return to the wall stile and continue directly up the bank to a track. Here go R to eventually pass through old mine workings following marker posts to the "Watkin Path". To return to Beddgelert from this location descend to main road and pick up paths passing to the south of Llyn Dinas. Instructions for this return can be found in the Rhyd-ddu to Beddgelert, via Cwm Llan walk from 6. onwards.

Refreshments: Beddgelert has a number of cafes and pubs supplying a range of food. The Antique shop and Bistro close to the bridge is an old favourite. However with such a choice it is worth investigating any of the other places.

Originally published in
Walks from the Welsh Highland Railway – Part 2

by Dave Salter and Dave Worrall

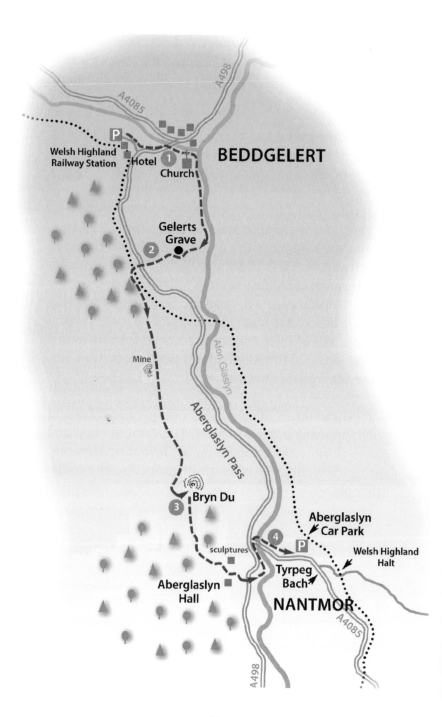

Walk 4
Gelert Path
(Beddgelert to Nantmor)

Walk details

Approx distance: *2½ miles/4 kilometres*

Approx time: *1¾ hours*

O.S. Maps: *1:50 000 Landranger sheet 115*
1:25 000 Explorer OL 17

Start: *From Beddgelert Welsh Highland Railway Station, Beddgelert.*

Access: *Behind the Royal Goat Hotel, on the A498 in Beddgelert.*

Parking: *Pay and display car parks at Beddgelert, Grid Ref. SH 588 481 and Aberglaslyn Grid Ref. SH 597 461.*

Going: *Good path through farmland and forest although the descent through the forest may be slippery under foot.*

The walk departs from the station at Beddgelert and passes close to the "Royal Goat Hotel". In 1802 the "Royal Goat" was built by a Thomas Jones. It quickly became one of Snowdonia's great hotels, offering guiding services for the wealthy up to Snowdon's lofty summit. Its name was not in fact the "Royal Goat" but the "New Inn" and it wasn't until the hotel received a visit from the King of Saxony in 1844 that the name of the hotel was changed.

Many walkers will be familiar with the legend of the

Gelert's grave on Glaslyn meadow

hound "Gelert", however for those who may not have heard the story the following is a brief resume. In the 12th Centaury Llywelyn ap Iorwerth, the Prince of Wales, whilst holding court in Beddgelert, would often take time to enjoy a days hunting in the nearby woods. On returning to their lodge after a successful days hunting, Llywelyn discovered his faithful hound "Gelert" covered in blood. Standing over his sons upturned cot and in a terrible rage, he feared the dog had murdered his son. Believing the worst he drew his sword and plunged it into the hounds great chest. As the hound lay dying, Llywelyn heard a cry from under the cot. With a pounding heart he lifted the cot to find his infant son completely unharmed. He then noticed that lying close to the cot was the body of a large wolf. In his anger Llywelyn had killed the dog that had fought and killed the large wolf thus saving his sons life. How bewildered the brave hound must have been to receive the sword instead of words of praise. With a heavy heart and deciding that "Gelert" shouldn't be forgotten, the faithful hound was laid to rest in a grave fit for a Nobleman, that grave still exists today for all to see.

Unfortunately this delightful, but sad story was a figment of the imagination of a number of villagers who in the late 1700's and early 1800's realised the need to encourage tourism to the area. David Pritchard, who was to become landlord of the "New Inn", along with a number of supporters for the project contrived to concoct the legend. The interest in the legend brought people from miles around to see the grave. The landlord and the villagers prospered from the increased numbers of tourists visiting and it could be said that the village is still benefiting today.

Ironically, in 1821 David Pritchard suddenly passed away at the age of 52, his death being so untimely that he had not even drawn up a will. Perhaps it was irony or a joke by Llywelyn's spirit that the instigator of one legend became one himself. Some weeks after his funeral, ghostly goings on were heard in the inn. All the villagers were held in the grip of fear. All that is, except his friend Huw. One evening whilst tending his cattle, Huw turned to find the ghostly apparition of his dear friend standing close by. With pounding pulse Huw was lead by the ghost to the inn where he was instructed to lift one of the great hearth stones. Under one of these he would find a purse containing a great deal of money and for returning this purse to David's wife he would receive the sum of two gold coins. He succeeded in locating the purse and he returned it to the innkeeper's wife and family. The ghostly figure has never since returned to the inn, but if you chance to indulge in the hospitality of the "Royal Goat Hotel" you may still hear David Pritchard's laugh when parting company with your money.

The walk passes the grave and memorial to the faithful hound and in the remains of a building can be seen the sculpture of a dog, presumably of Gelert, by the sculptor Rawleigh Clay.

The Walk: Depart from the station car park and walk down to main road. Turn L and along main road to bridge. Do not cross the bridge instead cross over the road. Go along riverside lane (signposted Gelert's Grave and Toilets).

1. Just before footbridge go R through gate (signposted Gelert's Grave) and follow path with river on L. At path junction turn R (signposted Gelert's Grave). Pass gravesite and continue on to small enclosure/ruin. This ruin contains a statue of Gelert. Exit ruin and turn R through wooden gate and into field. Cross to track and continue up to main road.

2. Cross main road and over railway track. After railway track continue along grassy track which is level at first. Pass through gate and into next field. Cross the field to a stile in the R.H corner. Over stile and continue ½ R between spoil heap and ruin. Path then gradually climbs up before finally reaching a viewpoint.

3. Exit viewpoint and return to path, now turn L. Soon, go over stile and into the forest. Turn L, descending the path, which follows way marker posts. Keep a look out for the remains of a miner's cottage on the L, which contains some interesting sculptures. Descend to a stream with a bridge and pass through hole in fence. Turn L and follow fence to main road.

Now L along road to a bridge. Cross this and go through kissing gate at end of bridge.

4. Turn R ascending steps with fence on R. Go through woods and descend into Aberglaslyn car park. Exit car park at main road and go along road. In a short distance turn L up a side road to Nantmor and the railway halt.

This walk can be made into a circular walk back to Beddgelert by joining the "Fisherman's Path" at point **4.** of this walk.

Refreshments: Beddgelert has a number of cafes and pubs supplying a range of food. On a hot day it would be difficult to resist ice cream from Glaslyn ices near the Pizza restaurant in the village centre. However with such a choice it is worth investigating any of the other places.

Originally published in
Walks from the Welsh Highland Railway – Part 2

by Dave Salter and Dave Worrall

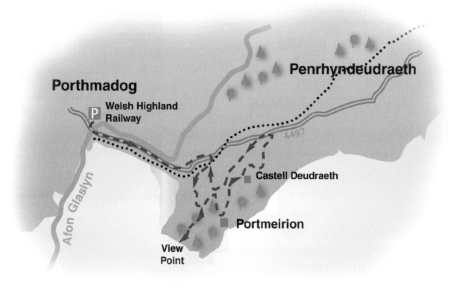

Walk 5
Porthmadog and Portmeirion Woodland

Walk details

Approx distance: *5½ miles/8.8 kilometres*

Approx time: *3 hours*

O.S. Maps: *1:50 000 Landranger Sheet 124*
1:25 000 Explorer OL 18

Start: *Ffestiniog Railway Station, Porthmadog*

Access: *Off the southern end of the main road in Porthmadog.*

Parking: *At Ffestiniog Narrow Gauge Railway Station and also close by at Grid Ref. SH 569 385 (pay and display).*

Going: *Paths are in woodland, open fields and lanes.*

In 1791 the Member of Parliament for Boston in Lincolnshire, William Alexander Madocks settled at Tan yr Allt close to what was to become the village of Tremadog. Being by nature an entrepreneur, the first of his many projects was to build and run a water powered woollen mill. This later became a laundry but unfortunately it later fell into dereliction and has recently been demolished. In 1800 he had started to reclaim some of the estuary near his home, which allowed him to venture into farming. During this period he realised that both agriculture and transport would benefit by reclaiming more of the estuary by building a barrage across its mouth. He was oblivious to the fact that such an action

Porthmadog harbour

Porthmadog Cob

would result in the loss of the fishing fleet located further up river at the mouth of the Aberglaslyn gorge.

In 1807 he commenced what must have appeared to most a very foolhardy project. By 1811 "The Cob" had not only been completed but had been opened to traffic. All for the cost in those days of £160,000. His success was to be short lived when the embankment was breached in a fierce gale. The locals, who must have believed in Madocks and his project, rallied around to collect funds to enable repairs to be carried out.

Since 1811 there has been a tollhouse at the Boston Lodge end of the Cob and a toll for this crossing was fixed by an act of parliament. This operated until 28th April 1978, when it was taken over by the Rebecca Trust who charged 5 pence for the privilege of crossing the Cob. It was also the cause of long and frustrating delays for the motorist. Money collected by the Rebecca Trust was given to local charities. At 09.15 on Friday 28th March 2003 the toll charge was taken away for good.

After the completion of the embankment Madocks continued to find new projects to keep him occupied; one such project being the construction of a harbour. This was to become Porthmadog and was completed in 1824. Almost at once, this started to serve the mines and quarries in the area, which were looking for the means to transport their goods to markets. In 1836, a narrow gauge railway line was constructed across the embankment to enable slate to be brought from the Ffestiniog quarries to the port. This in turn led to the construction locally of purpose designed Schooners, which were built and sailed from this quiet corner of Wales to ports all around the globe. These Schooners were affectionately known as Western Ocean Racers. They had sleek bows and sterns yet sported a bulbous

Traeth Mawr and Glaslyn estuary

amidships for maximum cargo carrying capacity.

Unfortunately due to the decline of the slate industry the Ffestiniog railway closed in 1946 and faced dereliction and the scrap mans blowtorch. With no prospect of the industry starting up again the railway faced certain closure. Fortunately in 1954 volunteers set up a trust to purchase the line and the remains of the rolling stock. In 1955 track repairs were under way and Boston Lodge Foundry was refurbished to commence the difficult renovation of those beautiful locomotives, which can be seen today. On the 24th May 1982 after many setbacks the line was re-opened to Blaenau Ffestiniog for the tourist trade.

The estuary is now a haven for bird watchers, especially with the return of the Ospreys to the area around Pont Croesor. Otter sightings have been reported close to the harbour in recent years.

The other well-known architect in the area is Sir Clough Williams-Ellis. Known primarily for the Italianate village of Portmeirion, he was also the designer of the original café on Snowdon's summit. Clough Williams-Ellis was born in 1893 into a distinguished Welsh family. From an early age he described the Welsh landscape as very dull and spartan and so to find solace in his lonely rural life he designed and constructed model buildings with basically anything he could lay his hands on. He studied Natural Science at Cambridge, later moving to London where he was to continue his studies under the guidance of his uncle, the Lord Lieutenant of Meirionnydd. It was his uncle who appointed the young Clough to become magistrate of that county, a position he was never to take up. Architecture was to dominate Clough's life, even though it could have been classed as eccentric. He was to design anything from cottages to war memorials, schools to churches; he even designed an upright grand piano. The completed object must have appeared monstrous and probably sounded worse.

It was to be Portmeirion that became Clough's claim to fame. The idea of the Italianate village came to him after his visit to Sorrento in Italy. After spending a number of years searching for a suitable location in such far away places as New Zealand, he was to eventually purchase land five miles from his home at Brondanw. The land, known as "Aber Iâ" (frozen river mouth) was owned by a relative of his, Sir Osmond Williams and was tenanted by a recluse, Miss Adelaide Haig. She had let the land become overgrown and neglected in order to keep visitors at bay but for Clough, this was just what he wanted. From 1925 for the next 50 years he cleared the land and in the process purchased adjoining

Portmeirion hotel

Portmeirion village and Castell Deudraeth

properties. He returned the mansion house to its former glory and opened it as a hotel, fortunately many of his guests were friends who never complained or were perhaps too polite to complain about the lack of electric and appalling food. The fact that neither Clough nor his staff knew anything about running a hotel and cheerfully acknowledged this fact did little to improve matters. The hotel was sadly gutted by fire in 1981, but with his typical love and devotion to his buildings he began a seven-year restoration project that would restore it to its former glory.

Clough was to buy up all types of derelict buildings and items from all over the world. He would move them to his project at Portmeirion but was to insist that no more than two buildings were of the same style. His Town Hall with its Jacobean ceiling, panelling and mullion windows were saved at the last minute from Emerald Hall in Flintshire. This provided the hall with excellent acoustics in which such musicians as Sir Arthur Bliss, Gerald Moore and Yvonne Arnaud have performed. The bandstand was an electricity substation and some of the paving slabs were the blanks cut out from slate lavatory seats. Even a statue of Hercules with a 1959 inscription on the base now stands majestically outside the Hercules Hall.

A number of notable people were to stay at Portmeirion. Noel Coward was to write "Blithe Spirit" in the fountain, George Bernard Shaw was to visit and one distinguished guest insisted he brought his entourage of "Bunny Girls" with him. It was thought to have been the location of Wing Commander Guy Gibson's last leave before he flew on the "Dam Buster" mission. The catalyst that brought Portmeirion to the attention of the general public was the 1960's cult TV series "The Prisoner" starring Patrick McGoohan. Clough decided to name his project Portmeirion because he considered it to be the Port of Meirionnydd. However, the only resemblance to a port in this brightly pastel coloured village is the concrete half boat constructed into the sea wall.

Clough received a Knighthood in 1972. He lived in nearby Brondanw with his wife Annabel Strachey, daughter of John St Loe Strachey, the Editor of "The Spectator". The house with its magnificent gardens is now looked after by his daughter. Clough died in 1973 at the age of 93. As is the way with many eccentrics, he wanted to mark his passing with a spectacular ending. He wanted to have his ashes packed into a firework rocket and fired over Portmeirion scattering his ashes in a most spectacular fashion. Sad to say his widow thought this was inappropriate and it's thought that his ashes were scattered in a much less spectacular manner.

Portmeirion is now looked after by a limited company and receives about 240,000 visitors per annum. The gardens at Brondanw are also open the public for all to enjoy.

The Walk: Start from the Ffestiniog Narrow Gauge Railway Station and head out along the Cob keeping railway on R. At end of Cob, close to engineering works (Boston Lodge) the path descends steps to the main road. Cross this and on to Cycle route. Now go R passing old toll house and to far end of lay by. Cross main road and up track (marked with a bridle way sign) to station (Boston Lodge halt). Cross over railway line and follow footpath through gate and into woods, with wall on L.

1. At fork go R following narrow grassy path passing through gate and up to a vantage point. From here there are spectacular views of Porthmadog, the estuary and also the surrounding mountains. Continue along path to pass through gate into field. Now go R along vague path (with fence on R) to pass through fence gap (gateway) close to farm.

2. Go R through small gate. Now ½ R up to viewpoint. Return to small gate and go L through fence gap (gateway), then R crossing field with fence and buildings on R to two gates. Through the R/H gate and along track.

3. At track junction (cattle grid in front) R down grassy path passing through gaps in two high walls and down to gate. Path now descends between wall and fence until the Portmeirion boundary is reached. L up path following footpath signs to gate with stile. Zig zag to R (this is the access to the Portmeirion entry kiosk and car park) Over stile and up field keeping as close as possible to L/H boundary passing under power lines. Through gate to join lane (Plas Canol on L).

4. At track junction, immediately before barn go R into field, path follows L/H field boundary (from this position more spectacular mountain scenery comes into view). Through gate and into woods, continuing with fence on L. Cross road and down lane passing bungalow on R. At T- junction, go L along lane and down to road (signs for Maes y Garth and Cae Eithin). L to main road.
5. L along main road to pass chapel and house Moel y Ddol on R. 75 meters after these properties L up lane. At track junction take L/H fork to pass between houses and

The cycle path near Boston Lodge

along to farmyard. Over cattle grid (same as location **4.**) and take R fork uphill. At Hafod Cae Maen continue to cattle grid (same as location 3.). Go R along track, which ascends for a short distance then descends between walls. When track swings sharp R and levels out, continue on through gate and down grassy path into woodland. Descend to Boston Lodge Halt. From here descend to cross the main road to join the cycle path. Continue along the cycle path (not the railway

track) back into Porthmadog. On this return section you may be able to view the bird life in the area. You may perhaps be fortunate enough to see the otters reputed to have returned to the area.

Refreshments: As well as the Ffestiniog Station restaurant there are a number of pubs and cafés in the area serving meals. At the north end of Snowdon Street is the famous fish and chip shop "Allports".

Entrance fees in 2009 for Portmeirion were £7.50 for adults. Contact them on 01766 772311 for opening hours.

Originally published in
Walks from the Welsh Highland Railway – Part 2

by Dave Salter and Dave Worrall

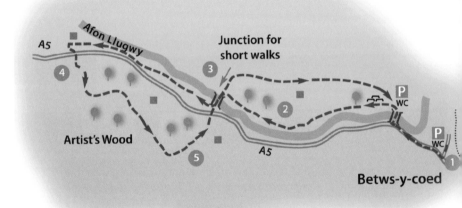

Walk 6
Artists' Wood, Betws-y-coed

Walk details

Approx distance: *2 miles/3.3 kilometres (or 4 miles/6.4 kilometres)*

Approx time: *1 hour or 1¾ hours for the longer walk*

O.S. Maps: *1:50 000 Landranger Sheet 115*
1:25 000 Explorer OL 17

Start: *Railway Station entrance in Betws-y-coed*
Grid Ref. SH 795 565

Access: *Betws-y-coed is on the A5. Both car parks are*
signposted. Trains from Llandudno and Blaenau
Ffestiniog. Buses from Porthmadog, Blaenau
Ffestiniog, Llangollen and Llandudno.

Parking: *Pay and display car park near railway station and*
at Pont-y-Pair.

Please note: *The path is narrow bear roots are slippery at times*
up to point 4.

Going: *This walk follows Afon Llugwy to the famous*
Miner's Bridge. From here you can walk back along
a lane or continue along the other side of the river
then return through the forest known as Artists'
Wood.

The beautiful landscape surrounding Betws-y-coed has attracted visitors since the early years of the 19th century when Thomas Telford built the Waterloo Bridge and the London to Holyhead road. This walk follows the picturesque Afon Llugwy to the well-known Miner's Bridge. The original bridge was built as a short cut for miners living at Pentre Du across the river who worked at lead mines on the plateau to the north.

The longer walk crosses the bridge and continues through woodlands on the opposite of the river for nearly a mile. The route then returns through Artists' Wood with its broad-leaved and coniferous trees. In the 19th centiury, many artists, including David Cox and Gastineau, used to visit Betws-y-coed and often painted in the vicinity of the wood. You will pass a stone that commemorates the planting of the first one hundred thousand acres of forest in North Wales by the Forestry Commission.

Walk directions: (-) **denotes Point of Interest**
1.   If parked near the station, have your back to the

railway station entrance and turn left to the A5. Turn right and cross Pont-y-pair over Afon Llugwy. Bear left and leave the lane, following the public footpath sign, to take a path beside the river. Both the path and broadwalk run parallel to each other. Where the broadwalk ends take a left at the fork joining the path. At the end of the trees walk through a kissing gate and follow the riverside path through a meadow.

2.   After small footbridge, walk through another kissing gate into trees and continue on a path until

44

you reach the Miner's Bridge. (For the short walk, do not cross it but go right uphill pass two wooden posts to a track and turn right to Pont-y-pair where you retrace your steps to the start.)

3. For the longer route, descend the Miner's Bridge to the opposite side of the river and go up steps. At the top turn right into the trees to meet another path, turning right to have the river below on your right. There are good views of the gorge below. The path descends to the riverbank but soon climbs again. Take care here on the slippery roots.

4. It crosses a footbridge over a stream and climbs over a little rock near the river. Stay on the main path and bear right at a fork. This path leads to some old mine buildings, follow the path around these and ascend to the A5. Notice the orange sediment on the opposite side of the river, proof of the metals within the earth.

5. Turn left for a few metres then turn right on a forest track with the name Maesnewyddion. After about 30 metres, go left on a narrow path. It soon curves to the right and goes uphill and turns to the left over stone steps. After about 50 metres, the path descends then rises beside a fence which it follows around a corner.

Artist's Wood

The Royal Oak, Betws-y-coed – a favourite with Victorian artists

The path then goes downhill to cross a wooden footbridge near the road. Continue up a few steps and on the path, passing the commemoration stone on your right. The path passes behind a house via two tiny footbridges, and, further on,  goes through tall trees before emerging on a track.

6. Turn left downhill and pass a parking area. The track becomes surfaced and passes houses. Bear left to cross the A5 to a footpath leading to the Miner's Bridge. Here you can retrace your steps to the start or, after crossing the bridge, go uphill to a lane then turn right to Pont-y-pair.

Originally published in
Short Family Walks in Snowdonia

by Dorothy Hamilton

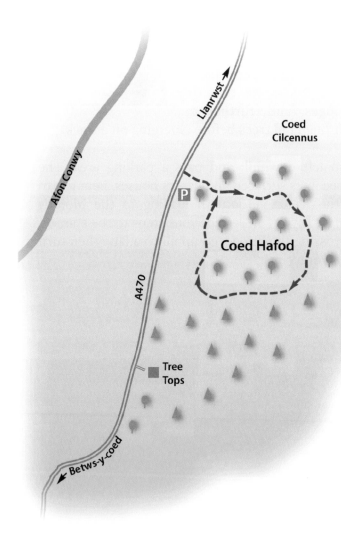

Walk 7
Coed Hafod

Walk details

Approx distance: *1½ miles/2.4 kilometres*

Approx time: *1 hour*

O.S. Maps: *1:50 000 Landranger Sheet 116*
1:25 000 Explorer OL 17

Start: *Grid Ref. SH 805 578*

Access: *By the A470, halfway between Llanrwst and Betws-y-coed. Coed Hafod is on the east side of the Conwy valley, halfway between Llanrwst and Betws-y-coed and can easily be reached on the A470. There is a convenient lay-by off the road approximately 2 miles/3.2 km south of Llanrwst and 2 miles/3.2 km north of Betws-y-coed. There are no particular landmarks to help you find the lay-by, though it is on your right shortly after passing the Field Centre and Tree Tops Woodland Climbing Centre if you are driving north from Betws-y-coed.*

Parking: *Lay-by on the north side (towards Llanrwst) of Tree Tops, the tree rope centre.*

Please note: *Woodland paths which can be steep and rocky in places, so walking shoes are recommended.*

Going: *Forest path during the whole walk.*

Site highlights
- Easy and attractive walk in mixed deciduous woodland.

49

- Excellent location for classic Welsh woodland birds like Pied Flycatchers, Wood Warblers and Redstarts.

Headline description

This is a beautiful area of mixed deciduous woodland, which provides easy walking on clearly signed and well-maintained footpaths. For the best birding experience, come here early on a spring morning to appreciate the dawn chorus, with Welsh

Footpath meanders through Coed Hafod

woodland specialists such as Pied Flycatchers, Redstarts and Wood Warblers, as you walk amongst the Bluebells and Wood Anemones.

Walk directions

Having parked in the lay-by, over the road from Rhyd-y-Creuau farm, walk a short distance north beside the road towards Llanrwst and turn right back on yourself up the woodland path.

This beautiful deciduous woodland can be enjoyed at any time of year, but to see and hear birds, it is best walked in spring. Birdsong will be at its peak at this time of year, particularly if you make an early start to appreciate the dawn chorus! Hearing the birds singing, and looking before all the leaves are fully opened, will make it easier to locate the birds. In spring, Bluebells and Wood Anemones carpet the ground at the edges of the woodland, and in the more open clearings.

Follow the path slightly uphill and climb two stiles in quick succession over a farm track between fields. The path continues to climb slightly, then bends round to the right and levels out.

You are now entering the heart of the woodland, and the noise of the traffic on the busy A470 becomes less intrusive. This is not a walk to be rushed; walk slowly and take the time to stop and listen. You will hear birdsong all around you, but after a while you will be able to tune out the more common birds and focus in on your target birds such as Pied Flycatchers and Wood Warblers. You may come across these birds anywhere on your walk, but here is a particularly good spot for these and Garden Warblers.

At the first junction, take the footpath on your left by the walk marker and follow this uphill. After a climb, the path levels out and you reach some old stone walls. In a slight clearing here, the path forks; take the right hand path which leads you between two stone walls.

The area to the right of the path here is particularly good for Redstarts and Wood Warblers.

Walk past the stone walls and follow the path as it climbs up slightly. You will shortly reach an area of beech trees.

Look and listen carefully for Hawfinches here. You may well hear the soft 'tic' call of the bird, but as it prefers the high canopy of the trees, you may find it frustratingly hard to spot the bird itself! Nuthatches are around, and you are likely to hear and see Great Spotted Woodpeckers without too much difficulty. Lesser Spotted Woodpeckers are also present here, but are considerably harder to see, though you may hear their almost raptor-like call. In winter you may see Bramblings in this spot.

The path bends left, and then continues fairly level in a roughly southerly direction at the top of the woods. After a while you will reach the end of the deciduous woodland; the other side of a stone wall sees the start of a conifer plantation. However, the path bends and descends quite steeply along the edge of the deciduous wood. At the bottom of the hill, where the path reaches a T-junction, turn right and follow the path beside the wall. The path bends through a gap in the wall and continues heading back to the start point.

You may be aware again of the A470 on your left and be able to hear the traffic, but that doesn't disturb the wildlife. This is another good stretch of woodland for Bluebells and Wood Anemones. Song Thrushes and Robins sing loudly to defend their territories, and Pied Flycatchers can also be seen along this stretch. You may catch sight of a Goldcrest, and even Firecrests have been recorded here in the holly bushes.

Ignoring the path that comes in on the right, continue retracing your steps to where you first entered the woodland. The path bends left and descends towards the two stiles. Cross these and one more to reach the road level and walk back to the lay-by.

What to look for ...
... in spring: This really is best as a spring walk. Almost anywhere along your walk in springtime you are likely to hear and see the specialist species of Welsh woodlands: Pied Flycatchers, Redstarts, and Wood Warblers. Lesser Spotted Woodpeckers are around but very elusive – you would be lucky indeed to see one, and you may hear, even if not see, Hawfinches in the tree canopy. Garden Warblers, Willow Warblers, Chiffchaffs, Blackcaps and Tree Pipits are also to be found here.

... all year round: Nuthatches, Treecreepers and Great Spotted Woodpeckers are relatively easy to find at any time of year, particularly in the area of beech trees. Goldcrests occur in some of the lower growing holly bushes, and even Firecrests have been found here.

Where to eat
Being equidistant from Llanrwst and Betws-y-coed, you are just two

53

Tree Top Adventure Centre

miles in either direction from a range of cafes, pubs, restaurants and hotels to suit all appetites and budgets. You have a much wider choice of facilities in Betws-y-coed, but this attractive village can be busy at weekends and holidays.

Other information
- Parking in roadside lay-by.
- No facilities on site, nearest public toilets in either Llanrwst or Betws-y-coed.

What other sights are nearby

- Attractive riverside centres of Betws-y-coed and Llanrwst.
- Gwydir Castle (privately owned but open to the public) and Gwydir Forest.
- Tree Top Adventure Centre – outdoor activities at a unique high ropes centre available to wide range of customers. Open 7 days a week with visitor centre, licenced bar and cafe, showers, car park. www.ttadventure.co.uk
- Conwy RSPB Reserve.

Originally published in
Birds, Boots and Butties: Conwy Valley/Eastern Snowdonia

by Ruth Miller

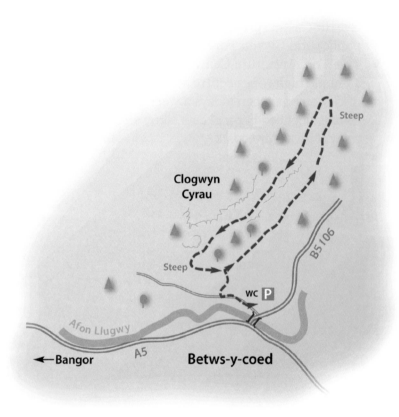

Walk 8
Gwydir Forest Park – Cyrau Walk

Walk details

Approx distance: *1.4 miles/2.2 kilometres*

Approx time: *1½ hours*

O.S. Maps: *1:50 000 Landranger Sheet 115*
1:25 000 Explorer OL 17

Start: *Pont-y-Pair car park*
Grid Ref. 791 567

Access: *Betws-y-coed is on the A5. In the village, turn off the A5 over the river for Trefriw. Immediately after the bridge turn left for the car park. Trains from Llandudno and Blaenau Ffestiniog.*

Parking: *Pont-y-Pair car park is pay and display.*

Please note: *WARNING. Weather conditions change very quickly on exposed routes, therefore we advise wearing suitable clothing and footwear, as well as carrying an appropriate map of the area.*

Going: *Steep climb up narrow path on entering forest. Also steep on the descent to join the track near the half way point.*

The Gwydir Forest Park stands at the gateway to the celebrated landscapes of glade, pool and crag familiar to generations of visitors who have walked the woodland paths and fished the clear waters of the Conwy, Llugwy, Lledr and Machno rivers since Victorian times. Above and beyond the valley slopes lies an extensive, rolling

Gwydir Forest

upland of wooded knolls, lakes and pastures, which stretches to the jagged Clogwyn-yr-eryr ridge.

The forest is made accessible by tracks, old miners' paths, cycle trails and long-established forest walks. These routes together with parking and picnic sites and details of nine specially waymarked walks have been brought together in this easy-to-read guide. We hope the publication will guide old friends and new on a pleasurable journey of discovery of the Forest Park.

Explore the Park

You can walk on any of the paths, tracks and forest roads except when forest operations necessitate temporary closure and diversions which will be signposted where possible. Further information about the Forest Park may be obtained at Y Stablau – the Snowdonia National Park Visitor Centre at Betws-y-

Gwydir castle, near Llanrwst

coed or from the Forest Office at Gwydir (Tel. 01492 640578).

The Forest Story

It is possible that the steep valley slopes at Gwydir have been wooded since post-Ice Age times, but scarcely any semi-natural woodland has survived centuries of exploitation. Records from the eighteenth century refer to the rafting of timber down the Conwy for shipment, and there is an account of horse-drawn wagons trundling huge oak logs all the way from Betws-y-coed to Anglesey. In 1778 the antiquarian Thomas Pennant, referring to Carreg-y-Gwalch just above Gwydir Uchaf, was told 'the noblest oaks in all Wales grew on this rock within living memory'.

The Forestry Commission began its work here in 1921, many hillsides had been stripped by the 1914-18

wartime fellings. The first task was to replant these areas. Oak, beech, larch, silver fir and the very successful Douglas fir were planted on the fertile lower slopes.

Much of the land was acquired for Lord Ancaster whose family inherited the ancient estate of the Wynns of Gwydir Castle.

The Wynns had long ago moved up the hill to Gwydir Uchaf, built by Sir John Wynn in 1604, it still stands, and is now a Forest Office. Sir John's role in the story is significant; he began the development of the mineral potential of his estate. This became the dominant industry of the Gwydir uplands for three centuries. Mining for lead and zinc reached a climax between 1850 and 1919. The legacy of old engine-houses, waste tips and reservoirs are characteristic features of the forest landscape today and several of the most important mines have been partially restored and made safe for visitors to see.

During the early days forest workers used to plant out millions of tree seedlings from the Diosgydd nursery, to protect and thin the crops, and to build roads needed for harvesting. The forest still gives direct employment to 75 people, and creates local work for many others.

Gwydir Forest has become familiar to thousands of

visitors who walk the paths, study wildlife, cycle, climb, canoe, fish, orienteer, or merely enjoy the calm of these timeless woodlands. Since 1993 the heartland of the forest has been accorded the special status of Forest Park.

Walk directions

Turn right out of the car park and follow the lane uphill. Ignore the public footpath sign onto a path. At the junction turn right follow the white arrows. These will be followed for the entire walk.

Follow the lane winding left passing wooden sign for Cyrau Walk. At fork bear right and immediately after follow white sign onto path into the forest. At a path fork take a right towards the viewpoint. Admire the view of Betws-y-coed and beyond, but be aware of the steep cliff beneath here.

Continue on the path through the conifers passing a path joining from the left. The path descends down to a path crossroads, take care here. At the crossroads turn right to follow the path onto a track. Bear right here. Follow this track down to the lane and back to the car park.

Originally published as a leaflet by the Forestry Commission

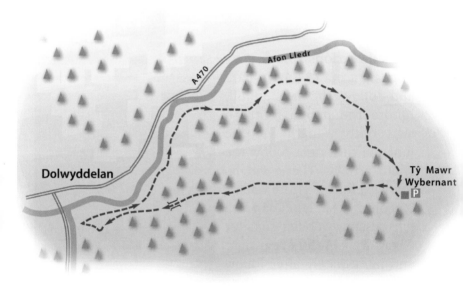

Walk 9
Tŷ Mawr Wybrnant

Walk details

Approx distance: *7 miles/11.3 kilometres*

Approx time: *3¾ hours*

O.S. Maps: *1:50 000 Landranger Sheet 115*
1:25 000 Explorer OL 17 and 18

Start: *Tŷ Mawr Wybrnant*
Grid Ref. SH 770 525

Access: *You can reach Wybrnant either from Penmachno or from the road between Betws-y-coed and Dolwyddelan after passing Fairy Glen. There is no bus service here, but you could go by bus to Dolwyddelan and begin your journey from there through the forest to Wybrnant and back over the mountain to Dolwyddelan.*

Parking: *Park your car outside Tŷ Mawr – there is space for about half a dozen cars there or in a small car park further up. There is no bus service here, but you could go by bus to Dolwyddelan and begin your journey from there through the forest to Wybrnant and back over the mountain to Dolwyddelan.*

Please note: *Tracks can be rough in places.*

Going: *Forest tracks and paths.*

Tŷ Mawr Wybrnant is situated in the Wybrnant valley near Penmachno and was the birthplace of Bishop William Morgan, the translator of the Bible into Welsh.

Tŷ Mawr, Wybrnant

The house has been restored to its probable 16th/17th century appearance and includes a display of Welsh Bibles and Bibles in other languages and an exhibition room. In the house behind Tŷ Mawr is an exhibition on the drovers.

The walk – from yr Wybrnant, over the mountain to Dolwyddelan following a possible old drovers' route and then back along the banks of Afon Lledr and through the forest to Wybrnant.

Go towards the house called Pwll y Gath (to the right of Tŷ Mawr) – turn left before you reach Pwll y Gath going through gate – and you will see a sign on a post. Follow it to a gate. Go through it and to the left, walking with the wall. Follow the track between two walls to a gate and stile. Go over it and then up the path that goes alongside the wall to a lane. Cross the lane and go straight ahead in the direction of Dolwyddelan. Follow the path alongside the wall to another lane. Cross it and go straight ahead along the path. It can be a bit wet here after heavy rain as with other parts of the path further along.

Go through the trees to a stile. Go over it and to the top of the hill. Follow the path along the flat moorland to a post in the ground and along the path with a large rock on the right. Continue towards another large rock with Foel Felan mountain on your right and keep left and then down towards a stile. Go over it and along the path through the trees. Follow the path through the forest. Continue ahead after crossing a  forestry track. Follow the footpath signs – you will come out of the woods for 300 yards. Keep to the path with a fence and a field on your right. You will then re-enter the forest.

You will come to a lane, turn left going over the stile next to the gate and quarry waste on the left. Go past an old quarry on your left to a gate and kissing gate. Go through the kissing gate and continue along the lane to a fence, gate and kissing gate. Go over the stile, past some houses on the left and to the right and to some bridges. Go over the railway bridge. Turn right and not into Dolwyddelan, but if you have the  time why not pop into the village? There are two hotels – the Gwydir and Elen Castle – and a shop there.

Go to the right past a school and further along Tŷ Isaf farm and to a gate. Go through 3 gates and walk along the banks of Afon Lledr. Bear left through a gate, keeping with the river. Don't go left over the bridge but keep straight ahead to a gate. Go through it and straight ahead along the wall, past a house on the right to a post in the field and straight ahead until you see a small tunnel on the right. Go through it under the railway and to the left to a stile

Cross the stile and continue along the lane. Go through a smaller gate and past a house on the left and you will see a stile on the right. Go over it and up the field with a stream to your right until you come to a gate. Go through the gate to a lane. Keep left and up the lane, past an agricultural building on the right and then down to a gate and stile. Go over the stile and continue along the lane, ignoring a path that comes up from the left. You will then see a path going to the right. Follow it through the trees, past a post with an arrow on it near a ruin and then straight ahead to a post that points right, up a very rough track and follow it to the left.

You will then reach a post with an arrow pointing to the right, follow it up a steep slope to a post with its arrow pointing upwards. Go through the trees, past four posts to a piece of level ground. Go past another post and through a gap in a wall to a stile and arrow. Go over the stile and keep straight ahead. There is no path now and you will have to walk through long, wiry grass, heather and bilberry bushes. Go straight ahead with a pine forest on your right (keep within about a hundred yards of the forest).

When you see a deciduous forest in front of you, you will come across a path. Follow it to the left, following a fence until you reach a gate. Go through it and into a field. Go to the right and you will find a gap behind a rock. Go through it and down the field along a poor track and to a bit of path that runs alongside a fence to a gate. Go through it and down through the trees to a small gate. Go through it and past Tan y Clogwyn to a lane. Go to the right and back to Tŷ Mawr.

Bishop William Morgan
A gifted scholar, he studied Hebrew, Greek and Latin at Cambridge University. He was priest of several northern parishes before becoming Bishop of Llandaff and later St Asaph. His greatest contribution was his great work in translating the Bible into Welsh, which he did at the behest of Elizabeth I. He finished the work in 1588 and from then on the Welsh could read the scriptures in their own language. This, say many, is what saved the Welsh language from extinction. The New Testament had already been translated into Welsh by William Salesbury in 1567, but Bishop Morgan's Bible gave the language a formal orthography and a standard written Welsh. His wide vocabulary and the poetry of the translation gave the Welsh a dignified language. Every Sunday, with the royal seal of approval, the Welsh people would hear this dignified language from the pulpits and this was a great contribution to the survival of the language.

Other Points of Interest

Afon Lledr It is a tributary of the Conwy, rising on Moel Siabod and joining the main river just outside Betws-y-coed. It is noted for its salmon and trout fishing.

Dolwyddelan Legend has it that a young woman called Elan, famed for her looks, wished her name and reputation to live forever. She declared: 'Not for nothing am I able to immortalise my name. If there is not any other land prettier than this, henceforth my name shall be upon it.' But the name of the village most probably came from St Gwyddelan, who founded a church here in the 6th century. The present church is reputed to have been built by Maredudd ap Ieuan ap Robert, a distant descendant of Llywelyn Fawr (the Great), who came to live here in the 1500s. Maredudd died in 1525 and is buried in the church, and there is a memorial to him and his family on the north wall of the church.

Dolwyddelan castle It is the birthplace of Llywelyn ap Iorwerth (Llywelyn Fawr). The earliest buildings are early 13th century. The castle covers two routes into Snowdonia, and it remained an important stronghold for his grandson, Llywelyn ap Gruffudd, but its capture by the English – perhaps through treachery – in 1283 was a turning point in the English campaign. It was immediately repaired and garrisoned by Edward I. The English maintained a military presence here until 1290, but their long-term strategy of control relied on military and administrative centres accessible by sea, and inland castles became increasingly irrelevant. The castle was occupied again in the 15th century, when it

Dolwyddelan castle

was leased to Maredudd ap Ieuan, who added an upper storey to the keep.

Drovers The export of store cattle from Wales to the rich pasturelands of England played a vital part in the Welsh economy from the mid-13th century onwards and by the mid-17th century cattle exports were one of the primary sources of Welsh revenue. The growth of urban populations during the late 18th century led to an increased demand for beef and thousands of Welsh cattle were driven into England for fattening after being purchased by dealers and drovers at local fairs. In 1794, 10,000 cattle were exported from Anglesey and by 1810 14,000 were being sent annually to the Midlands from Anglesey and the Llŷn Peninsula alone. Gentlemen employed drovers as carriers of money and news, and Welsh drovers pioneered the establishment of banks in west Wales.

The Welsh drovers who took cattle to London were

regarded by the townspeople with suspicion. An account of Barnet Fair in Farmers Magazine in 1856 refers in a rather uncomplimentary fashion to the Welsh drovers: 'Imagine some hundreds of bullocks like an immense forest of horns, propelled hurriedly towards you amid the hideous and uproarious shouting of a set of semi-barbarous drovers ... driving their mad and noisy herds over every person they meet if not fortunate enough to get out of their way ... the noisy "hurrahs" of lots of "un-English speaking" Welshmen ... to be seen throwing up their long-worn, shapeless hats high in the air ... uttering at the same time a ... gibberish which no-one can understand but themselves.'

The size of a drove of cattle varied according to the time of year and demand, ranging from one hundred to four hundred cattle attended by four to eight drovers and their dogs. It took three to four days for the drove to settle down to a steady two miles per hour, a pace which would give the animals opportunity to graze by the wayside. They would cover between fifteen and twenty miles per day so as not to force the cattle and and cause them to lose condition. A long and strenuous day over rough mountain track would be followed by a shorter day's travelling to give the cattle an opportunity to recuperate. The dealer or the foreman drover would ride ahead to arrange accommodation for both men and animals, at either farms or inns, many possessing paddocks where cattle could be held overnight.

The end came with the extension of the railway to Shrewsbury in 1856 and cattle being loaded into railway trucks for the remainder of the journey. Within a few years the railways had reached into Wales

Cwm Wybrnant

enabling the cattle to be carried all the way to the markets.

Originally published in
National Trust Walks 1. Northern Wales

by Dafydd Meirion

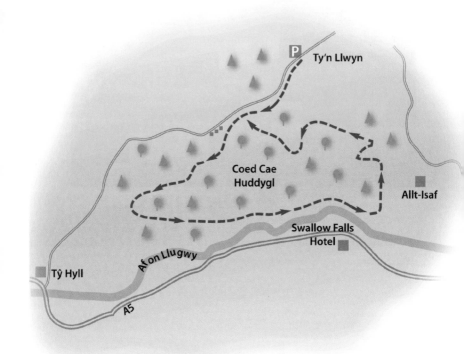

Walk 10
Swallow Falls

Walk details
Approx distance: *2½ miles/4 kilometres*

Approx time: *2½ hours*

O.S. Maps: *1:50 000 Landranger Sheet 115*
1:25 000 Explorer OL 17

Start: *Grid Ref. SH 763 583*

Access: *Take the narrow uphill road behind Tŷ Hyll for 1 km to reach Ty'n Llwyn car park.*

Parking: *Ty'n Llwyn car park.*

Please note: *Very dangerous at Point 3.*

Going: *Riverside forestry track, very steep in places.*

Walk directions

1. Start at Ty'n Llwyn. Walk down through a gap in the fence by the car park and follow the yellow-top markers down clear path.

2. After a sharp corner to your right, cross an old stone wall ruin. After 50m cross forest track and continue ahead downwards. On reaching another forest track take the track on your right, marked by the yellow signpost. Continue along the forest track – the Llugwy river will soon be on your right.

The foamy waters of 'Swallow Falls'

3. The path narrows, keep on ahead. Walk with the fence on your right. You can take a right here down the steps to see Swallow Falls, where there is a bench. Retrace your steps back up to the path and turn right to carry on with the walk.

This part of the walk is very dangerous, the fence has fallen in places, with a big drop. **Be careful!!**

4. At a fork where the fence stops take the left path. Turn left when coming to a wider path. On reaching a forest track turn right, following the markers. After 50m turn left up steps and continue upwards.

After a steep climb you can walk to a viewpoint – be careful of the steep drop.

Return to the path, go through a gap in the wall and carry on upwards back to the car park.

Tŷ Hyll

Afon Llugwy near Tŷ Hyll

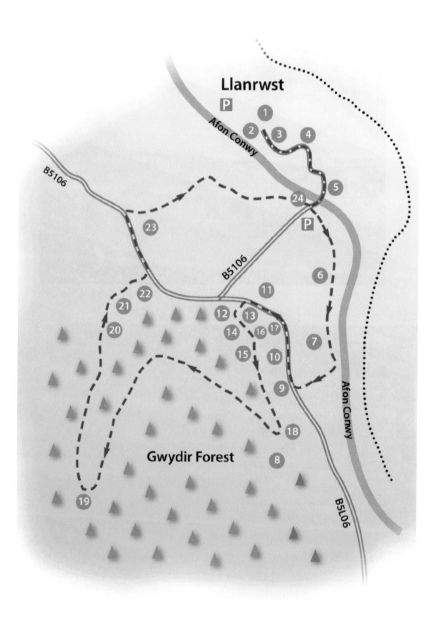

Walk 11
Walking with the Wynns of Gwydir

Walk details

Approx distance: *4 miles/6.4 kilometres*

Approx time: *2¼–2½ hours*

O.S. Maps: *1:50 000 Landranger Sheet 115*
                 1:25 000 Explorer OL 17

Start: *St Grwst's churchyard, Llanrwst*
                 Grid Ref. SH 797 616

Access: *From the town square, Llanrwst.*

Parking: *Park over the bridge on your left or behind Glasdir*
                 centre in Station Road, Llanrwst.

Please note: *Some forestry tracks and footpaths.*

Going: *Field paths and country lanes.*

Introduction

From the Statute of Rhuddlan of March 1284 until the Act of Union of February 1536 the Conwy Valley was controlled by English colonial administrators. By 1536 the Welsh gentry had proved themselves sufficiently sycophantic to be entrusted as agents of the English Crown. The Wynns of Gwydir eagerly sought and gained administrative office and royal patronage and before the close of the 16th century Sir John Wynn had established himself as the most powerful man in northern Wales. The family dominated Dyffryn Conwy and are still spoken of in glowing terms by some

Gwydir castle, Llanrwst

commentators, but as we walk in their footsteps around the places they knew well, we examine their reputation.

The Walk and Points of Interest

To reach Gwydir Chapel (1) from Ancaster Square (4) walk down the lane at the side of the Eagles Hotel, past the almshouses (3) and enter St Grwst's church (2). Continue through the main body of the church and turn right into the chapel.

1. Gwydir Chapel was erected in 1633-4 by Sir Richard Wynn and contains the remains of, and memorials to, many members of the family. In the east corner is a white marble setting out the elaborate pedigree of the family. Under the traditional Welsh political system clan and kindred were crucial. Loyalty and support were owed and given within enduring relationships of kinship rather than to a more abstract concept of the 'State'. Sir John Wynn (1553-1627) famously wrote a book that purports to be a family history but was

primarily intended to establish the Wynns as legitimate offspring of the Princes of Wales. The Wynns intended to exploit kin loyalty to enhance the family's value to the English establishment. Where the Welsh nobility had once rallied resistance to English domination, after the Act of Union the native gentry rushed to become more English than the English! The Wynns were particularly impatient to ingratiate themselves with the Crown. The Statutes of Union may have banned the use of the Welsh language from all official proceedings and documents, effectively making ordinary folk foreigners in their own land, but for the gentry it provided golden opportunities. The Welsh upper classes were enabled to become magistrates, merchants, courtiers or members of parliament. John Wynn ap Maredudd was the first of the family to scramble aboard the gravy train, becoming High Sheriff of Caernarfonshire in 1544-45, 1553-54 and 1556-57 and MP for the county from 1551 to 1553. He died on the 9 July, 1559 and is commemorated here by a small white marble tablet bearing a Latin inscription. His son, Maurice Wynn, was the first of the family to abandon traditional Welsh naming practice and adopt the English form of surname, as recommended to the Welsh by King Henry VIII. This was a powerful sign of where the family's new loyalties lay. The Wynns had abandoned the struggle for independence pursued by Llewelyn ap Iorwerth, whose stone coffin lies here an enduring reminder of more honourable times.

2. In the main body of the church is an exquisite oak rood screen separating the nave from the chancel. This screen, composed of intricately carved birds, fish, foliage and weird dragons, was pillaged from Maenan Abbey by the Wynns following the dissolution of the

monasteries. Besides this screen the squires of Gwydir 'acquired' tons of building materials and acres of land from the destruction of the monastery and its estates. However, when Sir John Wynn tried to also grab the tithe income of this church, Bishop William Morgan staunchly defended the rights of the rector. When Wynn, in 1604, turned the screws on him to hand over the cash Morgan wrote to a friend, 'I were better rob by the highway side than do that which he requesteth'. Morgan went on to describe Sir John Wynn as 'a sacrilegious robber of my church, a perfydiouse spoyler of my diocese and an unaturall hynderer of preachers and good scholers'.

3. These almshouses were erected between the winter of 1610 and spring of 1612 as part of the Jesus Hospital Foundation to accommodate twelve poor people, 'eleven men and one old woman for their bedmaker'. There are twelve single room dwellings, six on each floor, with those on the upper floor reached by stairs at the rear. The groundfloor apartment at the western end was made into a passageway in 1812 to give access to the warden's house, which was being remodeled. The almshouses were endowed by Sir John Wynn, who also endowed a grammar school in Llanrwst but didn't consider it good enough for his own sons who were variously educated at Eton, Westminster, Bedford, Lincoln's Inn and St John's College, Cambridge. Although these almshouses continued to shelter the needy for more than three centuries, they were consistently hampered by the determination of the Gwydir household to improperly channel income from the almshouse endowment into their own capacious coffers.

4. According to Sir John Wynn before the rise of his

family this square was run-down and deserted. His *History of the Gwydir Family* not only describes the scene, but identifies the culprit; 'for Owain Glyndŵr's wars . . . brought such a desolation that green grass grew on the market-place in Llanrwst called Bryn-y-boten and the deer fed in the churchyard of Llanrwst, as it is reported, for it was Owain Glyndŵr's policy to bring all things to waste, that the English should find not strength nor resting-place in the country'. This is spin-doctoring of a high order. Sir John's famous *History* is a masterpiece of self-justification. Having constructed a specious pedigree asserting the family's inbred superiority, the book seeks to illustrate the destructive folly of Welsh leaders who opposed domination by the English Crown. By implication, and in contrast, he suggests the collaborationist policy of the Wynns was delivering peace, prosperity and social advance. In reality the run-down state of Llanrwst owed more to the effects of the de-population caused by the plague than to Glyndŵr's scorched earth policy. The plague had also hastened the collapse of the old social order and created vacant landholdings, which were systematically appropriated by the Wynns.

After retracing your steps to Ancaster Square turn right down Bridge Street and continue over Pont Fawr (5). At the far end turn left and continue along the riverside path, passing through a kissing gate beside the football ground you soon catch sight of Gwydir Castle (6) behind the trees, with its characteristic tall chimneys across to the right.

5. Pont Fawr was built in 1636 to replace a bridge that 'had fallen into the greatest decay'. The costs of £1,000 were raised jointly by the counties of Denbighshire and Caernarfonshire, which it connected. Its elegant design

is often ascribed to Inigo Jones and although this is unproven, as Queen Henrietta Maria's Treasurer, Sir Richard Wynn was acquainted with the famous architect and may well have invited him to produce drawings for this project. When an enormous river pearl was discovered in laying foundations for the bridge the obsequious Sir Richard presented it to the queen who subsequently incorporated into the Crown Jewels.

6. The parkland of Gwydir Castle originally extended to the river. The oldest parts of the building date back to 1500, the time of Maredudd ap Ieuan ap Robert, Sir John Wynn's great grandfather, but Gwydir Castle now appears much as it did when Sir John took over in 1580.

Soon after passing a football ground on the right you notice some large blocks of stone along the river-bank and a wide flat topped wall (7) stretching across the fields to the right.

7. This raised, stone causeway, which encloses the southern flank of the castle gardens was constructed by Sir John Wynn in the 1590s and by the 19th century was referred to as the 'Chinese Walk'. Here at the badly-preserved eastern end was a quay built to receive supplies for Gwydir Castle. Sir John Wynn made Afon Conwy navigable as far as Gwydir for small ships and barges and surviving accounts show that he regularly

received supplies of spices, fine wines and tobacco from London, via Beaumaris. The Chinese Walk is altogether some 550 yards (500m) long, 7 feet high (2m) and 5 feet (1.5m) wide and at the Gwydir end concludes with a flight of eight slatestone steps.

Continue along the riverbank for 660 yards (600m) and immediately after crossing a stile turn right. Notice the rocky crag (8) looming up ahead (and slightly to the left) and follow the fence across the field over the stile, to exit onto the old Betws-y-coed road over the stile. Note the derelict structure (9) across the road opposite (and a little to the left).

8. The forested crag up ahead, 'Carreg Gwalch', concealed 'Old Siencyn's Cave', the legendary home of Dafydd ap Siencyn, Dyffryn Conwy's own Robin Hood. Siencyn was an historical figure whose later life is shrouded in mystery and legend. Descended on his mother's side from Llywelyn Fawr he was a Lancastrian Captain who fought to keep the Yorkist forces out of Nant Conwy but is best remembered as an outlaw and a poet. Numerous tales describe his expertise with bow and arrow and his forcible redistribution of wealth from rich to poor, an activity unlikely to endear him to the house of Gwydir! The Wynns somehow managed to acquire Dafydd ap Siencyn's spurs which hung for many years in Capel Gwydir (the sole surviving specimen can be viewed on application to the vicar).

9. Ffynnon Gowper stands abandoned and ill cared for. At some time known as Saint Allbright's spring, for centuries this was an important local source of drinking water. Almost two centuries ago it was improved by the Gwydir Estate. Thomas Roscoe recorded the details in his *Wanderings in Wales* (1836), 'At a bowshot from Gwydir Castle stands the fountain

of St Allbright. The stream which at this place offers its cooling waters to the lips of the traveller, as it issues through the stone conduit, is supplied by a large cistern constructed for that purpose at a considerable distance up the mountain. An open elevated court, of semi-circular form, stands close to the roadside, backed by a stone wall of corresponding figure, surmounted in the centre by pedimented blocks; a narrow channel perforated in the blocks opens a passage for the pure element, through which it issues all day long in one unceasing stream'. The Estate celebrated the official opening of the fountain with, 'A grand invitation to all the poor old men and women of the neighbourhood, who were plentifully regaled with tea and cakes, and flowing flagons of good ale, and sent merrily home at night with a small portion of money in their pockets'.

Turn right and continue along the road past the Capel Gwydir Uchaf sign to view Gwydir Estate cottages (10) and the entrance to Gwydir Castle (11). A little further on, by the Trefriw road sign, turn left through a sort of open doorway in the wall, ascend the steps and continue to follow the path (12) as it climbs the forestry hillside.

10.One and two Ty'n y Coed and Gwydir Cottage were built in the 19th century to house workers on the Gwydir Estate, and were usually occupied by gardeners. Gwydir Cottage is the earlier example, having been erected around 1845 in a picturesque 'Tudorbethan' style derived from the vernacular architecture of Capel Curig's Tŷ Hyll, known in English as the 'Ugly House'. Although the squires of Gwydir were no longer called Wynn, there was continuity of ownership. In 1678 Lady Mary Wynn had married Robert Bertie, Baron Willoughby de Eresby, who later became the first Duke of Ancaster, and the estate passed down through various Ancasters and de Eresby's until 1895 when it was sold to a cousin, Earl Carrington.

11. This is the main entrance to Gwydir Castle, the historic home of the Wynns (tour is worthwhile, if time permits). The family's great wealth and power and indeed their historical reputation rests largely on the shoulders of Sir John Wynn whose portrait hangs in a lower hall whilst his ghost is said to haunt the spiral staircase leading from the Solar Hall to the Great Chamber. A walled-up void within a chimneybreast is

claimed to have concealed the body of a young serving maid seduced and subsequently murdered by Sir John but such stories lack solid evidence. However history provides numerous well-documented examples of John Wynn's tyrannical behaviour. On his own admission he physically threatened his uncle, Owen Wynn and his tenants following land disputes in Gwydir and Trefriw in 1591. In the same year after a disagreement with William Williams of Cochwillan, his own clansman, he admitted to have given him 'a box on the ear'. Between 1580 and 1611 Sir John Wynn was involved in at least twenty-seven law suits involving fraudulent land transactions, forcible entry, rent abuse and corruption in office. In 1615 he was fined £1,000 for constantly harassing his Llysfaen tenants in an attempt to extract higher rents and it is claimed that he committed a woman to the stocks merely because her son refused to sell him land. Constantly on the lookout for cash he was accused in the Star Chamber of abducting rich widows as rewards for loyal followers and kinsmen, including his own brother, Richard Wynn. After surreptitiously pocketing public defence funds he was warned by the Lord President in 1591 that: 'I wolde have all men know that I do mislike such lewde dealinge'. When Sir John was permitted to purchase a baronetcy in June 1611 he proved reluctant to keep up the payments and by July 1613 was £365 in arrears. Receiving a written rebuke from the Privy Council Wynn nevertheless continued to ingratiate himself at Court and was proud to claim that he had kissed the Prince's hand, dined in the royal household and served as standard-bearer at a royal funeral. Defenders of the Wynns praise the family for continuing to sponsor the age-old bardic traditions of Wales, but for Sir John Wynn they had political value. Although the Welsh gentry were impatient to become part of the English establishment they were initially careful not to be perceived by their countrymen as having sold out. They retained a foot in both camps whilst it paid them to do so. By the time of Sir John's death in 1627 the Wynns had well and truly 'arrived', and demonstrated little further interest in Welsh culture. Since 1600 an increasing number of poems sung at Gwydir emphasised their patrons' connections with London! For the Wynns and their fellow high-born Welshmen, Union with England offered exciting opportunity; for the ordinary people of Wales it spelt abandonment.

12. This is 'Lady Mary's Walk', named after Lady Mary Mostyn (1585-1653), the daughter of Sir John Wynn.

This historic footway connects Gwydir Castle with its summerhouse and pleasure gardens on the hillside above. Despite neglect, the path retains several interesting features including revetting where necessary, steps at the steepest points and slate edging. The forestry may be modern but the path's rather gloomy aspect seems original as it was described in the 17th century as a 'low melancholy walk'.

The path zig-zags up the hillside but stay on course to emerge between Gwydir Uchaf (13), on the left, and Capel Gwydir Uchaf (14), on the right.

13. Although Gwydir Uchaf is an attractive building it was far grander when originally unveiled by Sir John Wynn in 1604. Originally, the Wynn's coat of arms stood above the entrance, surmounting the motto 'Utile Dulci' (Profit and Pleasure)! It is widely accepted that Gwydir Uchaf was erected to serve as a summerhouse for Gwydir Castle yet historian Mortimer Hart intriguingly suggests that Sir John may have intended it to serve wider political ambitions. Contemporary commentators described Gwydir Uchaf as 'the finest house in Gwynedd', which might add weight to Mortimer Hart's theory that Sir John was actually primarily intent on ingratiating himself with royalty by providing prestigious lodgings for travellers of noble birth or high station journeying to Ireland.

14. Capel Gwydir Uchaf must be viewed internally to be properly appreciated (free admission). Built in 1673 by Sir Richard Wynn (John's grandson) to serve Gwydir Uchaf, services continued to be celebrated here until 1920 with the rector of Trefriw paid a retainer to serve as the Estate's chaplain. The chapel's interior is dominated by a glorious painted ceiling which the Royal

Commission on Ancient Monuments claim is 'one of the most remarkable examples of this class of 17th century art in Britain'. Bingley, the 18th century traveller remained curiously unimpressed, 'this is a small building in the Gothic style, sufficiently neat on the outside, but the roof and some other parts are decorated with paintings of scriptural figures, most miserably executed'.

Continue walking to the enormous yew tree in the middle of the forestry yard (16) in front of Gwydir Uchaf and then glance into the nearby walled enclosure (17) now occupied by two modern houses.

15. Much of the area surrounding Gwydir Uchaf was originally laid out as pleasure gardens. The small hillock just west of the chapel originally formed a low ziggurat or ornamental mound. The term derives from the Babylonian temple-tower design where each tier was smaller than the one below, producing a pyramid effect. The edges of the tiers would be ornamentally planted and it is likely that a pathway ascended the mound, in helicoidal fashion, providing a viewing platform, or mount, as these were all the rage in 16th and 17th century pleasure gardens.

16. This yew tree is a rare surviving example of Gwydir Uchaf's 17th century ornamental planting. The stump situated nearer the building was probably another example. The surrounding car-park area is rubble-revetted to the east and originally provided a viewing platform.

17. Before the forestry insensitively planted these houses in its midst, this was a half-acre walled garden serving Gwydir Uchaf. A variety of soft fruit and vegetables were grown in this sheltered setting and it is quite possible that vines were cultivated here for the

production of the wine that records indicate were made by the estate in the 17th century.

Walk down the roadway overlooking Llanrwst on the valley floor to your left, leading in a southerly direction, away from Gwydir Uchaf. Turn first right, past a barrier. After about 80 yards (73m) turn sharp left and follow the forestry track for 600 yards (550m). Just before the main track bears right and turns back on itself you follow a short path to the left to reach a bench (18).

18. This bench marks the position of a Tudor bowling green that originally formed part of the Gwydir Uchaf pleasure gardens, indeed Sir John Wynn mentions playing bowls in a letter to his chaplain. The site was originally selected for its stunning outlook, which provides a particularly good view of the course of the raised walkway (7). Although the bowling-green long ceased to serve its original purpose it continued to be used for festive events by the people of Llanrwst until the years of the Second World War. It was subsequently largely obliterated by the Forestry Commission who drove the track you have just followed through the centre of the green.

Follow the forest lane around the hairpin and the sharp right bend and continue to gently ascend north-west for 500 yards (455m). Where the main track splits, take the smaller right fork track and continue on a fairly level contour until you pick up a series of yellow-topped marker posts. After 0.3 km the track narrows and soon you are able to see across the market town of Llanrwst and the eastern slopes of the Conwy valley. Follow the path straight

ahead, through the two wooden gateways, over the bike track. You begin to hear the sound of running water and notice a parallel path about 70 yards (64m) lower down

the hillside on the right. Carry on the path in front. When you reach a junction with another track, bear right and after 55 yards (50m) meet another junction where you turn right down a tarmac path which descends quite steeply. After 165 yards (150m) you turn left along a short footpath which passes a stile on the left and leads into an open, surfaced area (19).

19. Always alert to money-making opportunities Sir John Wynn was eager to profit from the exploitation of local minerals and this was the site of Parc, the largest and longest worked of the Gwydir mines. Mining began here in the early 1600s and only finally ceased in the 1960s. Sir John seems to have first contemplated exploiting local mineral wealth rights in 1611 when he sent two 'great pieces of lead' to the naturalist, Sir Thomas Chaloner, the younger. His researches continued until January 1620 when he leased the mineral rights of the Llanrwst 'wastes and commons' for 40 shillings a year. Failing to extract expected profits, in

1625 Wynn employed a spot of moral blackmail to induce Sir Hugh Myddleton to lend his expertise, 'I beg say to you as the Jews said to Christ, we have heard of they great works done abroad (alluding to the New River and other projects); doe somewhat in

thine own country . . . I have lead ore on my ground in great store and other minerals near my house, if it pleases you to come hither'. Although mining continued under the Wynns, it was in the 19th century that Parc expanded dramatically. One noted mining engineer who organised this more systematic approach to extraction was Captain Kneebone, whose name was bestowed on the dramatic cutting situated opposite the information board (accessed via above-mentioned stile). Although most of the workings scattered throughout the forest are 19th century, Sir John Wynn's pioneering role is widely acknowledged and he is often referred to as 'the father of mining at Gwydir'.

After investigating Kneebone's Cutting, return to the descending track where you turn left and continue for 1,000 yards (910m). Passing two barriers, after the second barrier bear right onto the road to reach Nant cottage (20) where you bear left, following the sign towards Llanrhychwyn, crossing the bridge over the small stream. Cross the ladder stile that soon appears on the right and descend the smaller path down the picturesque gorge, with its waterfalls (21) at the top before crossing a wooden bridge overlooking the curious abandoned ruins (22) at the bottom.

20. Nant was erected in 1845 to accommodate the head forester of the Gwydir Estate, who for much of the 19th century was a man called John White. Although most of the existing forest consists of coniferous trees first planted here in the 1920's (partly by conscripted armies of the unemployed) at the time of the Wynns it was almost entirely oak woodland. This was another resource the house of Gwydir was anxious to exploit. Although a certain amount of timber was sold locally, much of it was floated down river and exported via

Trefriw quay. By the mid 18th century this enterprise alone yielded almost ten thousand pounds a year!

21. This is Rhaeadr y Parc Mawr, also known as the Grey Mare's Tail; but does this particular mare not appear to possess two tails?

22. These are the remains of mill buildings that formerly served two economically important

industrial functions for the Gwydir Estate. Felin Blwm was originally erected to crush ore extracted from Parc Mine and could well be the lead mill listed in surviving 18th century estate accounts. Around 1900, with a general

decline in lead mining the works were converted into a sawmill and the estate's head forester appointed to also act as timber agent.

Turn left after exiting the gorge area through the large wooden gate and continue along the Trefriw road for 225 yards

(200m). Climb over a stone and wooden stile on the right, cross a footbridge over a stream (23) and continue to a wooden ladder stile at the far end of the field keeping with the fence on the left-hand side. Now you follow a delightful lane that provides glimpses across to Gwydir Castle on the right and a little further on an excellent view of the older parts of Llanrwst before arriving at the rear of Tu

Hwnt i'r Bont (24). Your original starting point is but a short way beyond.

23. This stream, the lower waters of Nant Gwyd, were intended to become the 'Trefriw Lead Canal'. To facilitate the transport of ore from Felin Blwm (22) to Trefriw quay, for onward shipment, the estate began to canalise the lower waters of Nant Gwyd. The project was seemingly abandoned around 1800, half-heartedly taken-up again in 1820 but never completed.

24. Tu Hwnt i'r Bont was built as a farmhouse in the early 17th century and served as a

Court of Sessions under the Wynns of Gwydir. Under the Tudors the responsibilities of Justices of the Peace comprised not only the enforcement of law and order but ensuring conformity to the established religion, the regulation of trade, commerce and employment, the maintenance of the poor and the upkeep of roads and bridges. The partiality and self-interest of the Wynns was

renowned and the quality of the justice they dispensed here characterised in verse by Thomas Pennant:

> 'When steel shod cattle crossed the ford
> And the valley ruled by a well-wined Lord;
> I stood a Court House, cold and grave

As dismal as old Siencyn's Cave;
On yonder crag I spelt the Law,
An object of pity, spile and awe
And many a knarled and trembling hand
In terror gripped the witness stand;
As empty-gloried tyrants sat
And on their fellow mortals spat;
Their bride-horned justice, dark the day
Where the Wynns of Gwydir held their sway.'

The Wynns played a key role in the history of Dyffryn Conwy, transforming traditional Welsh patterns of kinship loyalty into hierarchical subservience to the English State. Their enthusiastic anglophile 'modernising' brought the family great wealth and their tenants impoverishment and oppression. Indicted before the Council of the Marches Sir John Wynn, revealing the contempt in which the rising class of Welsh gentry now held their fellow countrymen, dismissed his accusers as, 'illiterate, simple people not having the English tongue'. As Edmwnd Prys, poet and contemporary of Sir John Wynne aptly observed:

'Bonedd a fwrian' benyd
Ar bawb o wrengwyr y byd . . . '
('The gentry slaps oppression on all the world's common people . . . ')

Originally published in
Walks in the Conwy Valley

by Christopher Draper

Tu Hwnt i'r Bont

Y Bont Fawr crossing Afon Conwy at Llanrwst

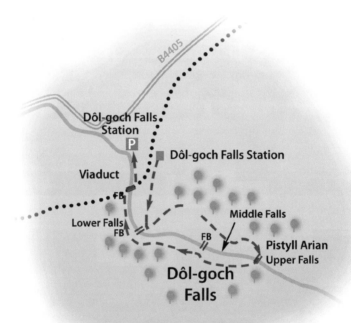

Walk 12
Dôl-goch Falls

Walk details

Approx distance: *2 miles/3.2 kilometres*

Approx time: *1–1½ hours*

O.S. Maps: *1:50 000 Landranger Sheet 135*
1:25 000 Explorer OL 23

Start: *Tal-y-llyn railway, Dôl-goch Falls Station*
Grid Ref. SH 649 047

Access: *On the B4405 there is a car park by roadside on the left before a sharp bend to the right when going from Bryncrug towards Abergynolwyn.*

Parking: *Car parkin front of Dôl-goch Station.*

Going: *Paths through attractive woodland visit viewpoints of three waterfalls. Some sections are steep and may be slippery when wet.*

Accessible only by footpath or train and located in woodlands, the station at Dôl-goch makes a fine starting point for visiting the Dôl-goch Falls. A feature of interest here is the three arch railway viaduct that spans the nearby ravine. The Lower Falls are close by and from there a footpath climbs the tree-clad slope to the Middle and Upper Falls. Keep a look-out for woodland birds

such as pied flycatchers. Where the stream flows placidly between the falls you may see dippers bobbing on rocks mid-stream.

Walk directions

1.   At Dôl-goch Falls Station ignore the Way Out sign and walk on a few paces to a wide path signed 'To the Falls'. Pass picnic tables and cross a footbridge over the line. Walk down the railed path, which has a fine view of the railway viaduct.

2. On reaching the river, turn left through a kissing gate. A viewing platform permits a good view of the Lower Falls. Walk back towards the gate but, before reaching it, bear right uphill on a stepped path. Take either path at a fork to pass Twll yr Ogof and continue with the river on your right. To follow the full walk, do not cross any bridges before reaching the Upper Falls.

3.   The path eventually ascends the hill by a series of zig-zags from which a seat offers views of the Middle Falls. At a junction bear right to reach the Upper Falls (Pistyll Arian).

4.   Cross the footbridge over the river. (If it is closed for any reason, return by your outward route.) Follow the path through the woods and ignore paths leading off it. Eventually you will drop down to the riverbank

at a point just beyond the Lower Falls. Cross the footbridge and turn right to retrace your steps to the station. Or, for refreshments, turn left to the Dôl-goch Hotel and Tea Room.

Originally published in
Walks from Welsh Heritage Railways

by Dorothy Hamilton

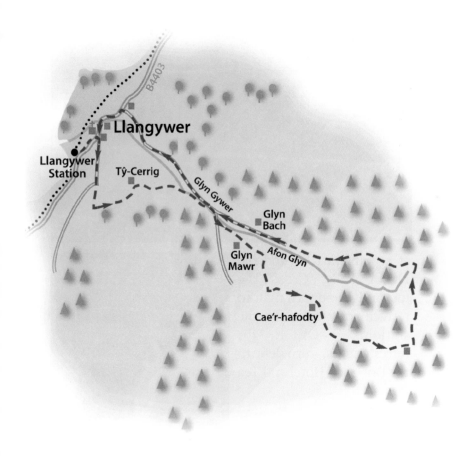

Walk 13
Llangywer

Walk details

Approx distance: *5 miles/8 kilometres*

Approx time: *2½–3 hours*

O.S. Maps: *1:50 000 Landranger Sheet 125*
1:25 000 Explorer OL 23

Start: *Bala Lake Railway, Llangywer Halt*
Grid Ref. SH 902 322

Access: *Follow Bala/Llanuwchllyn road, B4403 along*
southern side of Llyn Tegid to Llangywer.

Parking: *By Llangywer Station*

Going: *A long but gentle climb on paths and tracks through*
pasture and forest. The descent is along tracks and
lanes through Glyn Gower.

Llangywer is the only village on Rheilffordd Llyn Tegid (Bala Lake) between the stations of Llanuwchllyn and Bala. The 18th century church contains an unusual wheel-less funeral bier which was carried by having a horse at each end. Situated halfway along Llyn Tegid, Llangywer Halt is ideally located for picnics or watching birds. Herons, cormorants, ducks, grebes and other species may be spotted. Found nowhere else in Britain and possibly trapped here since the last Ice Age, a fish known as the *gwyniad* inhabits the depths of the lake.

Walk directions

1. From Llangywer Halt platform, walk out to the lane and turn left. In about 200 metres, turn right on a lane opposite the church. Pass a drive to Tŷ Cerrig and, where the lane bends right at a stream, cross a stile near a gate on your left.

2. Walk uphill with the stream on your left. Go

through a gap in a fence to enter another field and immediately go left downhill to a stile. Cross the small footbridge and take the path ahead, uphill. Do not take a path on the left that follows a fence but walk beside an old field boundary straight across the field that has a few trees alongside it.

3. Cross a ladder stile and bear slightly left downhill. Pass farm buildings on your left and bear right to cross two ladder stiles a few metres apart. Follow a fence on your left and, after crossing another stile, continue along a track bordered by trees. Go downhill to a stile and walk on to meet a forest track.

4. Turn left to cross a bridge over Afon Glyn and go over stile. Walk up to the lane and turn right. Ignore a lane on the left and cross the river again. In about another 50 metres, where the lane bends right, walk ahead along a track to pass a converted chapel on your right. Go over stile. Continue along a grassy track with the river and forest on your left.

5. Follow the track around to the right. When approaching a cottage on the right, bear left away from it to have a field boundary on the right. On reaching a

fence directly ahead, bear slightly right uphill (look back for fine views). In about 200 metres veer left with the track to go through a gate opening and follow the track to the buildings of Cae'r-hafoty.

6. Pass Cae'r-hafoty on your right and bear right to find an old track bordered by trees. Follow it through an old field boundary then veer half left beside a line of trees. Cross a damp area to another line of trees and walk ahead to a gap in a fence. Turn left to cross a stile at the edge of the forest.

7. Veer slightly right on a path through heather and coniferous trees. In almost 400 metres, at a footpath and bridleway junciton, bear left beside an area of felled forest. Cross a stream and continue ahead to some ruins. Walk between the ruined buildings and pass an old cottage.

8. Join a better track and bear left downhill to emerge on a forest track. Turn left and, in 100 metres, ignore a bridleway on the right. In a few more metres, at a junction of tracks, go left downhill.

9. The track crosses a stream and becomes surfaced as it descends through Glyn Gywer. In about 1.5 kilometres it emerges on the lane walked earlier. Bear right and either cross the bridge to retrace your steps over the hill, or follow the lane to the B4403. Turn left for approximately 400 metres to Llangywer Halt.

Originally published in
Walks from Welsh Heritage Railways
by Dorothy Hamilton

Walk 14
Dyffryn Maentwrog / Llyn Mair

Walk details

Approx distance: *2½ miles/4 kilometres*

Approx time: *1¾ hours*

O.S. Maps: *1:50 000 Landranger Sheet 124*
1:25 000 Explorer OL 18

Start: *Car park at Llyn Mair*
Grid Ref. SH 653 414

Access: *From Porthmadog follow signs for Penrhyndeudraeth and then the A487 towards Tan-y-Bwlch. From Blaenau Ffestiniog follow the A496. Here turn up towards Rhyd for approx. a kilometre.*

Parking: *Small car park at Llyn Mair is free of charge.*

Please note: *These walks traverse land owned today by six bodies; Snowdonia National Park, Ffestiniog Railway, The National Trust – Wales, Countryside Council for Wales, UPM Tilhill Forestry Ltd and the Woodland Trust. Also the private landowners of Bryn Mawr and Hafod y Llyn respectively. Only the generous goodwill and co-operation of all these parties has brought this footpath network into being. Please respect their property.*

Going: *Mostly forest tracks with slight hills that cross the railway. Path around the lakes can be slippery at times.*

Welcome to the Dyffryn Maentwrog/Llyn Mair footpath network which is extensive and includes over 30km of paths. The network was established for your enjoyment in 1989 by a partnership of local landowners and the numbered posts at path junctions will help you to find exactly where you are on this map. Enjoy your walk!

History

Much of the romance of exploring these paths is discovering, among the rich variety of wildlife and habitats, those tell-tale signs which show the area's rich historical heritage. Look for:

• **old estate paths** some dating back to the eighteenth century when the Maentwrog valley was landscaped by the Plas Tan y Bwlch estate.

• **the river Dwyryd**, visible from several viewpoints, originally ran through a network of saltmarsh channels on the floor of the impressive glaciated Maentwrog valley. The land was claimed for agriculture in 1797 and the river henceforth confined between dykes which snake their way from one side of the valley to the other.

• **forestry roads and tracks**, old and new oak was commercially grown here in the eighteenth to nineteenth centuries primarily for the ship-building industry at Porthmadog from where slates were exported all over the world. Some conifers were also grown for the quarries at Blaenau Ffestiniog, which were the main source of income to the Oakeley family of Plas Tan y Bwlch. The present conifer plantation dates from the 1960s.

Plas Tan y Bwlch

Coed Mawentwrog from Plas Tan y Bwlch

Coed Maentwrog

Llyn Mair

- **the Ffestiniog railway** – from 1836 carried slates from Blaenau Ffestiniog to Porthmadog. Today its trains, mostly steam hauled, carry tourists, and also provide a link at Penrhyn, Plas Halt and Tan y Bwlch stations for walks in the footpath network.

- **the old road through Rhyd** – part of which was a Roman road (Sarn Helen), drove road and one of the main coach roads through the area.

- **remains of stone walls and buildings** related to agriculture, forestry, gamekeepering and, in the area of Penrallt, old lead mines.

- lakes – Llyn Mair was built in 1889 and Llyn Hafod y Llyn is from the same period. The Millpond in the gorge below Llyn Mair once supplied water to power the estate saw mill, flour mill and a turbine which generated electricity for the Plas and village of Maentwrog. Llyn Trefor to the west was a drinking water reservoir supplying houses downslope.

Wildlife

The Maentwrog oak woodlands are managed as reserves by a number of organisations because of their wealth of wildlife. In addition the woodlands in the valley are recognised as being of European importance by being designated as a Special Area for Conservation (SAC) because of the large extent of upland oak woodland. This special habitat provided ideal conditions for mosses, liverworts and lichens and the rare bats that are found in the area. Notably the lesser horseshoe bat has its European stronghold here.

Birds – spring and summer are extremely good in the oak woodlands for pied flycatchers, redstarts and wood warblers as well as excellent numbers of our more familiar brids, while Llyn Mair over the winter is a magnet for wild ducks. Other birds recorded here are nightjar, goshawk and osprey.

Animals – fox and badger signs are plentiful, but remember that nine species of bats and the elusive pine marten have also been recorded here.

Plants – the most important element is the fantastic diversity of mosses, lichens and ferns growing on the oaks. Hundreds of different species are found here and their wonderful combinations of colours and forms are truly amazing.

Welcome and enjoy!

Walk directions   **(-) denote Point of Interest:**
From the car park go right to walk through gate on the opposite side of the road. There are picnic tables here. Follow the track bearing right.

Ascend gradually through gate until forking left at signpost 26. Follow the gravel path through a gap in the wall to enter Hafod y Llyn. This forest is managed by the Woodland Trust.

Pass a small pond on the right and continue on the path around Llyn Mair. At signpost 10 turn left to join track. Ignore the path on the right, but in a few metres turn right at signpost 11.

Shortly on the right there are

four steps next to a Beech tree. Follow these to a path, bearing right. Ascend steep path to a stile and cross the railway. Follow the steps through gate and bear right up the path. Pass a house on the left.

On joining a track turn left, and shortly turn right at a junction in front of a house. Pass a path joining from the left and at signpost 6 bear right to join other track. Here losing activity is obvious.

At a fork bear left with the railway below on the right. Ignore two path on the right and at signpost 30 bear left to continue on the track above Llyn Hafod y Llyn.

A few metres after passing signpost 16 on the left, follow a path on the right. This completes the circle around the lake and re-joins the track at signpost 30. Here bear left and after a few metres descend on a track on the left. Cross stile at signpost 21 and cross railway.

Bear left at fork near signpost 28 and again at signpost 27. Descend track back to the start via a gate.

Paths climb up to Tan y Bwlch station from the car park. Here there are toilets and a shop.

Originally published as a leaflet

by Dyffryn Maentwrog Footpath Working Group 2009

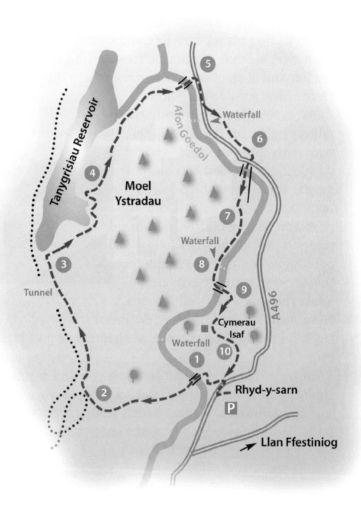

Walk 15
Y Dduallt – Tanygrisiau Reservoir (Llyn Ystradau) – Afon Goedol – Y Dduallt

Walk details
Approx distance: *5½ miles/9 kilometres*

Approx time: *4 hours*

O.S. Maps: *1:50 000 Landranger Sheet 124*
1:25 000 Explorer OL 18

Start: *Ffestiniog Railway, Y Dduallt Station*
Grid Ref. SH 678 421

Access: *By rail, from Porthmadog or Blaenau Ffestiniog*

Parking: *At any of the stations on Ffestiniog Railway*

Going: *Forest and moorland paths; one steep climb.*

Moorland to Tanygrisiau Reservoir followed by forest paths, waterfalls and a steep climb back to Y Dduallt Station.

Walk directions
The spiral at Y Dduallt was built because the original line near Tanygrisiau had been submerged by the hydro-electric pumped storage scheme. The deviation from the original track bed raises the line 35 feet, and goes through the new 287 yards tunnel before passing behind the power station to rejoin the old line at Tanygrisiau. The Queen opened the power station in 1963. Water released from Llyn Stwlan, a corrie lake

below the Moelwyn mountains, drops 300 metres to drive the generators. During the night, when the demand for electricity is low, water from the reservoir is pumped back to Llyn Stwlan by using electricity from the National Grid.

Near the lake, the walk passes the site of a granite quarry below Moel Ystradau. Worked from about 1919 to the 1930s, it produced macadam for roads. Further on, from the forest track, a house can be seen below, close to Afon Goedol. It is the old Dolwen power station that supplied electricity to nearby quarries and Blaenau Ffestiniog in the early 20th century. After passing Cymerau waterfall, the walk enters Woodland Trust land where many flowers, including wood sorrel and wood avens, are present in spring. The old farmhouse called Cymerau Isaf dates from the 16th century.

Walk Directions:

1. Park at Rhyd y Sarn. Go over bridge and take left immediately after bridge and go through the gate following the track and footpath to another small gate before arriving at the river. Follow the riverside path to a footbridge.

2. On the track now, go on an old track bed and bear right along it. In about another 200 metres, bear left along a track that passes closer to the present line. On your right is the entrance to the old tunnel. Go uphill and ignore other tracks on the right and then on the left. Pass through a gate (or over a stone stile above on the left) and follow the track downhill to have views of Tanygrisiau Reservoir.

From y Dduallt to Tanygrisiau

3. Ignore a stile on the left next to the railway line. In a few more metres, take a narrow unclear path on the right, before the lake. It heads in the direction of a quarried hill that has pylons crossing it. In about 400 metres it descends slightly near an inlet of the lake. Go

uphill towards a forest before heading left to a level area above a ruin on the right. Follow a fence but, in about 50 metres, veer left away from it to reach a track.

4. The track bears right, then left, to pass the quarried hill. Pass under cables coming from the power station and go left to have a marshy area on the right. The path rises a little to a fork. Bear right to cross a stile in the wall.

5. Follow a path which bears slightly left through bracken and heather. Pass some marshy ground on the right and a stony hill on the left. Descend to a wall and follow it on your left to a footbridge. Walk up to a kissing-gate and road.

6. Turn right along the grass verge. Pass houses on the left and a cottage on the right. In a few more metres, go through a kissing-gate on the left and slant right uphill to the right over boggy ground and slabs of rock. The path soon improves and runs parallel to the road. At junction, keep right. Descend gently through bracken to a track near a cattle grid. Bear right through a kissing-gate.

7. Cross the road and turn right. In about 100 metres, turn left along a track. Cross a bridge over Afon Goedol and ignore a descending track on the left. Walk uphill and pass a house on the right.

8. Bear right a few paces then go left onto a path through kissing gate. Continue on path through woodland and which soon runs near a river before veering further into the woods once again. Take a path

The path follows the southern side of Llyn Tanygrisiau
(left bank in this photograph)

Llyn Tanygrisiau with the power station

The waterfall in Coed Cymerau

Coed Cymerau

through more trees to a path junction. Turn left on the track to a footbridge but, before crossing it, turn left to the waterfalls.

9. Cross the bridge and continue along the path. Where it bears left, go through the small gate ahead onto Woodland Trust land of Coed Cymerau. Walk through deciduous trees to a track junction at a garage. Turn right along a track and follow it into a field. Before reaching a restored longhouse, bear left through a gate.

10.Pass a barn on the left and go through a kissing-gate. When the path turns left, bear right to a stile. Go downhill on a narrow path to join a wider path near a wall. Turn right downhill to a stile. Descend to the river and turn left through the gate and retrace your steps back to Rhyd y Sarn.

Originally published in
Walks from Welsh Heritage Railways

by Dorothy Hamilton

Walk 16
From Maentwrog to Rhaeadr Du
(Coed Felenrhyd)

Walk details

Approx distance: *6 miles/9.5 kilometres*

Approx time: *3½–4 hours*

O.S. Maps: *1:50 000 Landranger Sheet 124*
1:25 000 Explorer OL 18

Start: *Park in layby, Grid Ref. SH 663 402, 100m past*
footpath sign on left at edge of wood.

Access: *From A496, Maentwrog/Harlech*

Parking: *Going south from Maentwrog on the A496, park in*
laybay on the right (663 402). 100m past footpath
sign on left at edge of wood.

Going: *Paths normally dry and good.*

This walk is now maintained by Coed Cadw, the woodland trust for Wales. It has an information board which includes a map at the start of the walk. Extensive views over the sylvan Vale of Ffestiniog are a feature of the earlier stages of this walk. After an encounter with the hydroelectric power station's pipeline, a delightful woodland path snakes up beside the tumbling stream. On the way short detours lead to spectacular sights

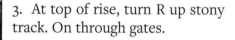

from both the top and bottom of the falls – Rhaeadr Du. An easy track brings you back to a lane which winds back round pleasant hills and hummocks.

Walk directions

1. Go up footpath, then ⅓L through gate and past houses.

2. Turn R up road.

3. At top of rise, turn R up stony track. On through gates.

4. At cylindrical building, bear L along small path (SE) twoards pipeline. It goes down to join larger path.

5. Down over stile to gate. Follow track L under pipe and at once R.

6. Fork R between houses. Soon R along road.

7. Go L over stile and down field to cross next stile. Follow path which bears R and soon U-turns L.

8. Detour R at fork to see falls and return. Ignore small L fork into pines. Take the next clear L fork into pines, but first detour R to see top of falls and return. Keep on when path joins yours from L.

An old pack-horse bridge by the power station

9. On over stream and stile. Fork L 30m to stile at wood edge.

10. Turn R up field and L at wall gap. Go up field with fence on your L.

11. Over that pipe and on along track.

12. Go L along lane.

13. Fork R.

14. Bear L at next road junction. Return the way you came.

Originally published in
New Walks in Snowdonia

by Don Hinson

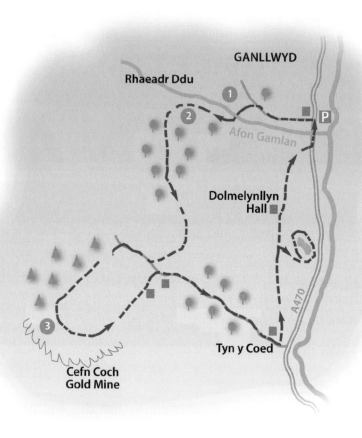

Walk 17
Ganllwyd – Rhaeadr Ddu – Coed Ganllwyd – Cefn-coch Gold Mine – Dolmelynllyn – Ganllwyd

Walk details

Approx distance: *4 miles/6.5 kilometres*

Approx time: *2–2½ hours*

O.S. Maps: *1:50 000 Landranger Sheet 124*
1:25 000 Explorer OL 18

Start: *Car park at Ganllwyd*
Grid Ref. SH 726 243

Access: *Ganllwyd is on the A470, north of Dolgellau. The car park is on the southern side of the village. Buses from Dolgellau and Blaenau Ffestiniog*

Parking: *Car park at Ganllwyd*

Going: *Easy/Moderate – woodland and hillside paths, tracks and lane*

Points of Interest:

1. The poem is by Thomas Gray and the original inscription was carved into a nearby rock. Thomas Gray is better known for his 'Elegy Written in a Country Churchyard'. William Alexander Madocks (1773-1828), who lived at Dolmelynllyn, may have been responsible for the carving. Many poets stayed at Dolmelynllyn and visited the waterfalls, which are on the estate. Madocks, keenly interested in landscape

design and town planning, created Porthmadog, Tremadog and The Cob embankment.

2. Rhaeadr Ddu is sited inside Coed Ganllwyd, a nature reserve. The spray from the falls and the high rainfall provide ideal conditions for mosses, liverworts and ferns. This is an ancient oak woodland, and the dominant tree is the sessile oak with some ash and birch. Alder buckthorn grows on the reserve, providing food for the caterpillars of the uncommon yellow butterfly, the brimstone. Look and listen for pied flycatchers, jays and other woodland birds.

3. The third richest of the Meirionnydd gold mines, Cefn-coch operated between 1862 and 1914. Gold was discovered in the Mawddach valley during the 1840s, when the Cwm-heisan mines (near Gwynfynydd in Coed-y-Brenin) were being worked for lead. A yellow metal caught in the dressing machine was identified as gold. The gold belt stretched from near Barmouth, east along the Mawddach estuary to Bontddu, and then north almost to Trawsfynydd. At first, ore at Cefn-coch was processed at the stamping mill near the stream. Later it was taken downhill by tramway to Berthlwyd, where the plant had a steam engine. Unfortunately, the workings became unproductive and the company wound up in 1866. The mine was worked again briefly, ten years later. The next revival was in the 1890's when a new company built a large mill. The ore was carried from the main adit by a level tramway. Almost 1,400oz of gold had been extracted when the mine finally closed in 1914.

Walk directions: (-) **denotes Point of Interest**
1. From Ganllwyd car park, walk across to the

information board and follow a path to the A470. Turn left and, before crossing the bridge over Afon Gamlan, turn right onto a gated lane.

2. In about 200 metres there is a lane junction, keep to the left lane. Follow the lane uphill and on a right turning bend take the footpath to the left through the trees to a markerpost, then keep ahead on a narrow path to a view of the falls, Rhaeadr Ddu, at a stone inscribed with a poem (1).

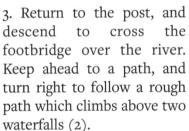

3. Return to the post, and descend to cross the footbridge over the river. Keep ahead to a path, and turn right to follow a rough path which climbs above two waterfalls (2).

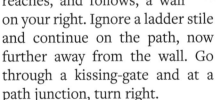

4. Look for a marker post and a path to the left that enters the woods. The path reaches, and follows, a wall on your right. Ignore a ladder stile and continue on the path, now further away from the wall. Go through a kissing-gate and at a path junction, turn right.

5. In about 25 metres, turn left through a gate and cross a footbridge. Bear right, uphill, to a

lane. Turn right, go through a gate and continue about 80 metres to take a grass track on the left. In a few paces, at a fork, go left again.

6. When a forest road is met on the right, ignore it. Keep to the left, on the track nearest the wall. Shortly, cross a stile and plank bridge on the left. Follow the path to a marker post on a wide track.

7. Turn left to pass the ruins of Cefn-coch gold mine (3). On the right is the crushing mill and on the left are

the barracks. Continue to a high ladder stile on the left. Cross the stile and descend the field, following marker posts. Cross another stile in a wall, and keep ahead to a small ruin. Pass it on your right and cross a stile near a gate. Continue to a lane.

8. Turn right to pass Berthlwyd, and follow the lane downhill for about 500 metres to a house called Tyn-y-coed. Immediately after passing the house, turn left through a small gate and follow the left fence to a gate that leads into woodland.

9. Follow the path down through another kissing gate, and reach a track. Here, a diversion can be made to visit an ornamental lake. Turn left after kissing gate and follow path downhill untill you get to a markerpost for the lake. Turn right here before turning left

to take the path around the lake, and cross a footbridge before returning to the track.

10.After visiting the lake, make your way back to the track following it straight ahead past Dolmelynllyn Hall. Follow the lane downhill and continue on the drive to the A470. Turn left to the starting point.

Facilities:
Guide available for exploring the Dolmelynllyn Estate, which is owned by the National Trust. Toilets in the car park at the start. Full facilities in Dolgellau.

Originally published in
Circular Walks in Meirionnydd

by Dorothy Hamilton

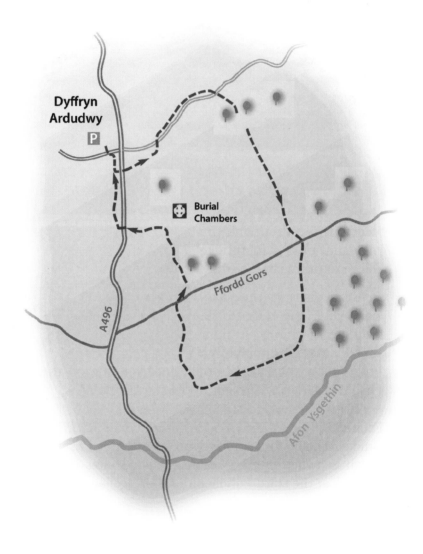

Walk 18
Dyffryn Ardudwy

Walk details

Approx distance: 2.5 *miles/4 kilometres*

Approx time: *1½ hours*

O.S. Maps: *1:50 000 Landranger Sheet 124*
1:25 000 Explorer OL 18

Start: *Grid Ref. SH 586 232. Car park in Station Road near the crossroads and shops in Dyffryn Ardudwy. Bus stops nearby.*

Access: *Dyffryn Ardudwy is on the A496 between Barmouth and Harlech. Buses from Barmouth, the Oakeley Arms at Maentwrog and Blaenau Ffestiniog. Dyffryn Ardudwy is on the Machynlleth-Pwllheli Cambrian Coast railway line. The station is about half a mile from the start of the walk.*

Parking: *Car park in centre of Dyffryn Ardudwy – on your right when travelling from Harlech towards Barmouth*

Going: *Field and woodland paths with several stiles of different types. On the return, the walk passes the Dyffryn Ardudwy Neolithic burial chamber. Quiet lanes.*

This fairly easy walk explores the attractive, varied countryside around Dyffryn Ardudwy. After a short, uphill stretch on a path and lane, the route passes through woods as well as fields offering extensive coastal views. Look out for spring and summer flowers.

The Neolithic burial chamber, passed near the end of the walk, consists of two chambers dating from about the 4th millennium BC. The lower, smaller chamber is the older and both have a capstone. Excavation in 1960 revealed ceremonial offerings of broken pottery near both chambers and in the larger tomb were Bronze Age cremated bones. The older chamber had its own cairn and, after the erection of the larger tomb, a huge cairn was built to enclose the two tombs. The burial site is of the portal dolmen type, which is also found on the east coast of Ireland.

Walk directions:

1. Leave the car park and turn left to the A496. Cross it, bear right and, after a few metres, go left on a track. It narrows into a path between a wall and fence then goes uphill to emerge on a surfaced track. Turn left to a road.

2. Walk uphill along the road and pass a road on the right called Bryn Awelon. Look on your left for a cemetery. A little further on, at a footpath signpost on the right, go up steps and through a small gate. Follow a path towards trees.

3. Climb a ladder stile in a wall and bear right through the trees, following a path that curves left away from the wall to meet a wider path. Bear right on the path through the woods and follow it to a stone step stile. Ignore the path going left and climb the stile. Follow the path ahead through a long field to a broad gate and lane.

4. Cross over the lane and climb a stone stile in the wall. Walk ahead, slightly right, to a stile near a gate and cross the field to the next stile. Continue ahead towards trees. Before reaching them, you will have a fence on your right.

Climb a stile and follow the right-hand fence to a little footbridge over a stream and continue through the trees with the fence on your right. When a track comes in from the left, continue beside the fence as it bends right. At another corner, head towards a small footbridge over a stream and follow the path to a small gate and emerge on a lane.

5. Follow the lane downhill towards the sea. Further down, go through a gate across the lane and pass below overhead wires. Before reaching houses, climb a stone stile on the right. It has a little gate on the top. Veer right to a small gate on the left and cross a wide wall.

Continue to steps and a small gate. On the other side of this wall, go right beside the wall and through a gate. There are farm buildings across to your right. Slant right up the field to join a track. Bear left, passing buildings on your right and go through a gate across the track.

6. Emerge on a lane and cross directly over the lane and through a gate into a field. Slant right uphill to a wall then continue with the wall on your right. Cross a broken wall and climb a stone stile in a corner. Cross a stream and follow a path downhill through trees to a gate in the left corner. Go ahead, slanting left through a field to a small gate.

7. On your left are the Dyffryn Ardudwy burial chambers. Lower down the path, a kissing-gate gives access. After visiting the site, continue on the path to a small gate and the A496 road. Turn right along the pavement to the start.

Originally published in
Short Family Walks in Snowdonia

by Dorothy Hamilton

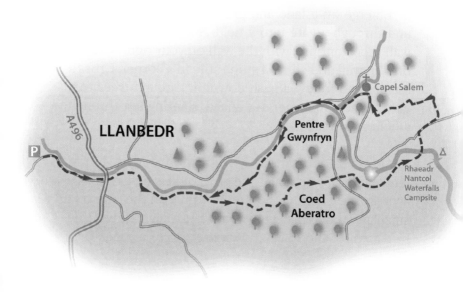

Walk 19
Llanbedr – Aberartro Woodlands

Walk details

Approx distance: *4 miles/6.2 kilometres*

Approx time: *2 hours*

O.S. Maps: *1:50 000 Landranger Sheet 124*
1:25 000 Explorer OL 18

Start: *Llanbedr bridge on the A496*
Grid Ref. SH 585 268
Grid Ref. SH 599 181, Llanbedr Station

Access: *Llanbedr is on the A496, south of Harlech. Car park near the railway station and on street parking in the minor road past the Victoria Inn. Llanbedr is on the Machynlleth-Pwllheli Cambrian Coast railway line. Buses from Barmouth, Blaenau Ffestiniog and the Oakeley Arms at Maentwrog.*

Parking: *Follow the directions to Llanbedr train station from Llanbedr Bridge. Continue 500 metres to a free of charge car park on the right. There are no toilet facilities at the car park.*
Grid Ref. SH 581 269

Going: *Hillside, woodland and riverside lanes and tarmac road*

This is a delightful walk through mature woodlands to pasture offering open views towards the Rhinog mountain range. The return passes Capel Salem, known for its famous painting.

Coed Aberartro is a mature woodland of beech, sessile oak, birch and other deciduous trees. In the spring you may spot flowers such as wood sorrel, wood avens and dog mercury. The path goes above an impressive gorge and crosses Afon Cwmnantcol to lanes and fields with beautiful views of the surrounding countryside.

The walk passes **Capel Salem** where you can see copies of the famous painting made by Curnow Vosper in 1908 of the chapel's congregation. The painting was shown at the Royal Watercolours Society Exhibition in

London and was bought by Lord Leverhulme. Since then the original painting has hung in Port Sunlight art gallery. Before the chapel was built in the mid 19th century, baptisms were carried out in a pool of Afon Artro below the chapel. (GR: SH 602 273)

Walk directions:

1. From the opposite end of the bridge to the Victoria Inn, go through a metal gate and take a footpath down steps to have Afon Artro on your left. Go through a kissing-gate and with trees on your left. Pass a children's playground and walk through a field to a kissing-gate. Turn right along the hedgerow and soon go through a gate to have a wall on your left. At buildings, bear left through a broad gate and walk through a farmyard, and then follow the farm drive to a lane.

2. Turn left and you will soon have the river below on your left. When the lane forks, veer right and walk uphill through woodlands. Ignore footpaths on the left and right. At a

house, the lane curves to the right and left to a fork. Take the left-hand track and go through a gate. Ignore a path on the right and walk through along the main track. After it curves to the right and passes a short section of wall, ignore a track on the left and walk uphill to a lane.

3. Cross directly over the lane and follow the track ahead. Take extreme care if you leave the route to descend to the bridge on the left for a view of the gorge. Continuing along the track, go through a gate across it and walk above the reservoir. Go through another gate then left at a fork to cross a footbridge

over Afon Cwmnantcol. Walk through a patch of woodland and approach an access track which leads to a campsite. Continue up the steep hill to reach a lane, passing the campsite entrance on your right.

4. Turn right and go through a gate next to a cattle grid. After about 100 metres, go left on a path enclosed by walls to a small gate. Follow the left-hand wall downhill and around a left-hand corner. At the next corner, climb steps in a wall then continue beside a left-hand wall.

5. Bear right downhill before a gate, then left, gradually going downhill beside the wall to a gate. Walk through the middle of the field to a wall then bear right beside it. When the wall goes left, maintain your direction beside trees, to reach a small gate. Continue ahead.

6. Turn right along the lane and, after a few metres,

you will see Capel Salem [2] on your right. The lane enters woodlands and descends to a cattle grid and another lane. Turn right over the bridge then left on another road. Follow it for 250 metres to Pentre Gwynfryn and, after another 80 metres, go left down steps to cross a footbridge over Afon Artro.

7. Bear right on a path beside the river. It becomes a track and passes a farmhouse. Ignore paths off it and follow the track to the fork in the lane walked earlier, and then retrace your steps to the start of the walk.

Originally published in
Short Family Walks in Snowdonia

by Dorothy Hamilton

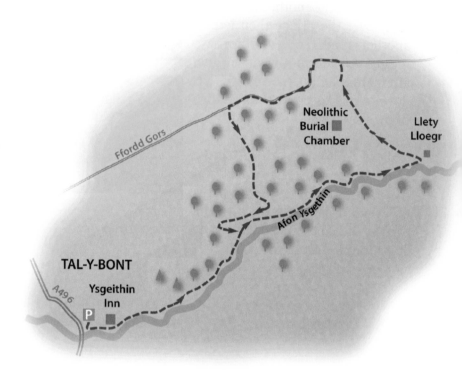

Walk 20
Tal-y-bont (Meirionnydd)

Walk details

Approx distance: *1.25 or 4 miles/2 or 6.4 kilometres*

Approx time: *1½–2 hours*

O.S. Maps: *1:50 000 Landranger Sheet 124*
1:25 000 Explorer OL 18

Start: *Grid Ref. 589 218. Tal-y-bont car park off the A496 opposite 'Tony's Italian Restaurant' and near the bridge over Afon Ysgethin*
Grid Ref. SH 589 218

Access: *Tal-y-Bont is on the A496, north of Barmouth. Buses are available from Barmouth, Blaenau Ffestiniog and the Oakeley Arms at Maentwrog. Bus stop is near the car park*

Parking: *The small car park is in the village centre on the left before crossing the bridge, when travelling from Harlech to Barmouth. The car park is free of charge and toilet facilities are available*

Going: *Woodland and riverside paths and a quiet lane passing a Neolithic burial chamber*

Points of Interest:

[1] This fine walk follows the tumbling **Afon Ysgethin** through the attractive Cors y Gedol broad-leaved woodlands. Bluebells, wood sorrel and other woodland flowers can be seen here in spring. For several centuries, Cors y Gedol was the home of the Vaughan family who involved themselves in local government.

[2] On the route you pass the **Ysgethin Inn**, a former woollen mill.

[3] After leaving the river, the walk emerges near **Llety Lloegr**, which was once a lodging and shoeing station for drovers taking Welsh cattle on the long journey to markets in England.

[4] Further along the route, the **Neolithic burial chamber**, locally known as Arthur's Quoit, stands on the left side of the lane. It is said that King Arthur threw the large capstone from the top of the hill called Moelfre and the indentations on the stone were made by his fingers. Some of the stones have fallen and the capstone rests on two side stones. Originally, the chamber would have been covered with earth and stones.

Walk directions:
1. From the car park, walk towards the river and go left on a track to have Afon Ysgethin [1] on your right. Pass

the Ysgethin Inn [2] and follow a path beside a wall. Pass a building on your left and you will soon be beside the river again.

2. Ignore a footbridge and go through a small gate. Continue beside the river and ignore another footbridge. The path rises a little and passes through an area of moss-covered boulders between deciduous trees. Cross a stile or go through a gate before approaching a small footbridge. On reaching a point close to the river, the path climbs quite steeply to emerge on a broad track with steps. (For the short walk, go left and ignore a track on the right, then continue with the directions at point 7.)

3. Turn right and follow the track gradually downhill, with the river below on your

right. The stoney track eventually runs close to the river for a while. When the path splits, ignore the path on the left and continue beside the river to a gate. The path soon becomes narrow and boggy and climbs to emerge on a lane opposite Llety Lloegr [3].

4. Turn left along the lane and follow it through grassland, trees and gorse. Take in the picturesque scenery where the mountainous farmlands meet the sea. After 300 metres you will see the Neolithic burial chamber [4] on your left. Continue along the lane and go through a gate across it and turn left.

5. Follow the lane around a left bend, ignoring a footpath on the right. Pass Cors y Gedol Farm and a house called Llysfaen on your right. Further along, where a drive leaves it for Cors y Gedol Hall, the lane bends left between tall trees. After 200 metres, go left through a gate by the footpath sign.

6. Walk along the broad, walled track and go through a gate across it. Ignore the immediate path on your right but, after a few more metres, you will reach a fork. Here, go right to have a stream on your right for a short distance. You will reach a junction of paths near a right-hand fence. Bear left, ignoring paths off. Follow a broad track between overgrown walls. On reaching another track, turn right. This is the point where you join the short walk.

7. Follow the track downhill, with Afon Ysgethin below on your left. Cross a level footbridge over a stream and go through a gate across the track. Join an access lane and pass bungalows on your right. Emerge on a road, but leave it immediately by going left through a gate to pass Llwyn Ynn Cottage on your right. Have a fence on your right and rejoin the  path beside the river. Turn right to retrace your steps to the start.

Originally published in
Short Family Walks in Snowdonia

by Dorothy Hamilton

Walk 21
Afon Clywedog – Torrent Walk – Brithdir – Afon Clywedog

Walk details

Approx distance: *3½ miles/6 kilometres*

Approx time: *2 hours*

O.S. Maps: *1:50 000 Landranger Sheet 124*
1:25 000 Explorer OL 23

Start: *Small lay-by on the B4416 to the south-west of Brithdir, Grid Ref. SH 761 181.*

Access: *3km east of Dolgellau, leave the A470 to take the B4416. Cross a bridge over Afon Clywedog, and continue to a layby on the left. The A470 is on the Machynlleth-Dolgellau bus route.*

Parking: *Small lay-by near the start of the Torrent Walk.*

Going: *Easy – woodland path above river, lanes and tracks.*

Points of Interest:

1. Thomas Payne designed the Torrent Walk, and also the long embankment across the estuary at Porthmadog. There were two paths, one on each side of the Afon Clywedog ravine, but the other has been lost through erosion and extreme plant growth. The walk was commissioned by Baron Richards (1752-1823) of Caerynwch, as an extension to the mansion's gardens.

2. The Afon Clywedog rushes and tumbles through

broad-leaved woodland of oak, beech, ash and lime. In about 300 metres, and close to beech trees, look for a bench overlooking the river. Provided by the North Wales Wildlife Trust, it is a memorial to the local botanist Mrs Mary Richards (1885-1977) of Caerynwch. With Peter Benoit she wrote *Contribution to a Flora of Merioneth* (1963) but she also travelled extensively abroad, especially in Africa, where she collected specimens for Kew. In recognition of her botanical work, she was awarded with an MBE in 1969.

3. A Roman road goes through Brithdir, which has a small Roman fort. To view the fort (which has no public access, but is visible from the road), continue to the village. Ignore the left descending road, but keep ahead on a lane. The site is on the left, a flat square with ramparts on the eastern side.

4. St Mark's Church, Brithdir, was built in 1885 after the death of the Rev. Charles Tooth, who was founder and chaplain of St Mark's Church in Florence. He wanted all his possessions to be sold after his death and the proceeds used for the Christian Church. His widow, Louisa Tooth, had already inherited property in Brithdir, and she carried out her husband's wishes by the building of this church. Although built of local stone, the style of the church is Italian. One of the architects was Henry Wilson of the art nouveau movement. The domed blue ceiling contrasts effectively with the red ochre of the sanctuary and chancel walls. The doors are of teak, and the lead font has a medieval design. Most remarkable is the beaten copper which has been used in the making of the pulpit and altar, thought to be the only ones so treated in

Wales. The Spanish chestnut choir stalls are decorated with carvings of animals. Mrs Richards was responsible for the planting of the rhododendrons in the churchyard.

Walk directions: (-) **denotes Point of Interest**
1. From the lay-by, return along the B4416 in the direction of the A470. Pass a lane on the left, and continue to a footpath signpost on the right. Go through a kissing-gate, signposted Torrent Walk (1).

2. Turn right over the bridge and follow the wide woodland path above the tumbling river, Afon Clywedog (2).

3. Emerge on a lane and turn right and continue on the same lane past the houses. Ignore a lane on the right, going uphill. (The usual return to the start of the Torrent Walk.)

4.   When the lane bends sharply to the left, keep ahead through a gate and follow a track. Go through another gate, and continue through the forest to a fork. Ignore the left descending track, which crosses a cattle grid. Keep ahead a few paces, then bear right uphill, through the forest.

5.   At a fork, keep on the track with a wall on the left. The track becomes grassy. Go ahead through a gate and follow the track to another gate. Keep ahead on the access lane to the B4416, and turn left in the direction of Brithdir village (3).

6. Pass a chapel and immediately turn right. Follow this lane past Cefn-y-maes untill you get to Ty'n-llidiart. Here continue on a grassy track to a gate. Cross to another gate, and walk along the clear track uphill.

7.   Go through a gate on to a walled track, and follow it to a lane.

8.   Turn right on the lane, downhill, to the B4416. Turn right to the lay-by at the starting point. Continue along the road for 300 metres if you wish to see St Mark's Church (4).

Facilities:
Cross Foxes Inn 1.5km south on the A470. Full facilities
in Dolgellau.

Originally published in *Circular Walks in Meirionnydd*
by Dorothy Hamilton

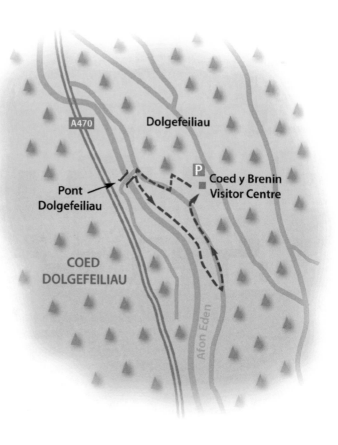

Walk 22
Coed y Brenin – Afon Eden Trail

Walk details

Approx distance: *1 mile/1½ kilometres*

Approx time: *45 minutes*

O.S. Maps: *1:50 000 Landranger Sheet 124*
                   1:25 000 Explorer OL 18

Start: *The Coed y Brenin Forest Park Visitor Centre. The entrance to the Afon Eden Trail is easily seen on the right when walking from the car park.*
Grid Ref. SH 723 268

Access: *From Dolgellau, take the A470 towards Porthmadog; turn right to the well-signposted Coed y Brenin Forest Park after going over a bridge to the north of Ganllwyd. Coed y Brenin Forest Park is accessible by bike along the SUSTRANS route 8/82. Route 8 from Dolgellau joins a quiet B road to the visitor centre. Bus 35 travels from Dolgellau to the visitor centre's car park.*

Parking: *Large Pay and Display car park at Coed y Brenin Forest Visitor Park*

Please note: *Walk is suitable for all – resting benches at least every 150 metres and no steps or stiles*

Points of Interest:

Coed y Brenin Forest Park covers an area of some 9,000 acres around the valleys of the rivers Mawddach, Eden, Gain and Wen. The rugged Rhinog Mountains lie to the west and the wild and lonely Rhobell Fawr to the east.

This was once part of the historic **Nannau Estate**, founded by Cadwgan, Prince of Powys in 1100 AC. The Forestry Commission bought it in 1922, and today Forestry Commission Wales looks after the forest for the benefit of people, wildlife and timber production.

Coed y Brenin was designated as a Forest Park in the 1990s because of its outstanding walking and recreational potential. Waymarked trails are offered to discover Coed y Brenin's rivers, hills, waterfalls, and woodlands with huge trees. Walkers will get a taste of this area's history and culture along them.

Set within Snowdonia National Park, Coed y Brenin Forest Park has everything from children's play areas to **world-class mountain bike trails**. Coed y Brenin made its name as Britain's first purpose-built mountain bike centre. If you haven't brought your bike it's not a problem as there is quality bike hire on site – best to book in advance.

Coed y Brenin **café** is the ideal spot to recharge yourself after being out in the forest. Take in the views down the valley to the Cadair Idris range.

Walk Directions:
The trail follows the river Eden climbing through the forest of young oak, rowan, birch and beech.

1. Start outside the Visitor Centre shop and café and go right where you will see a large sign directing to the Afon Eden Trail.

2. Walk along past a play park on your right and continue through the wood track. Along the route you can enjoy a virtual ranger tour with MP3 audio trails

which give information on local heritage and wildlife.

3. Follow the slopping trail to a bench. Proceed downhill and turn right, following the pathway. At the bottom of the trail, cross a track to rejoin the trail which will lead down to Afon Eden.

4. Follow the winding path and as you approach MP3 post '5' you will see a bridge on your right _ Pont Dolgefeiliau. The linear route which is suitable for wheelchairs ends here but the riverside loop route continues from here. By the river is a picnic site suitable for all.

5. Leaving the picnic area, the trail gradually gets steeper. Approaching the end of the trail will be a wooden gate by a bench. Go through the gate and turn left and take the path on the right. Continue ahead towards the Visitor Centre.

Best Walks in Wales

A series of guide books to take you to every corner of this magnificent walking country

- Short family walks
- Excellent coastal walks
- Hill and mountain walks & panoramic views
- Level lakeside and valley walks
- Woodland and nature walks
- Fascinating heritage and history guides
- Clear coloured maps
- Route photos and attractions on the way
- Updated directions

www.carreg-gwalch.com

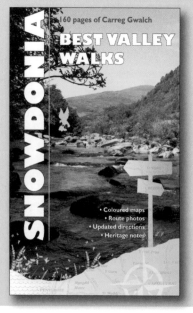

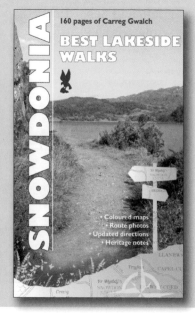

First published in 2015

ISBN: 978-1-84524-196-4

Cover design: Carreg Gwalch

Published by Gwasg Carreg Gwalch,
12 Iard yr Orsaf, Llanrwst, Wales LL26 0EH
tel: 01492 642031
fax: 01492 641502
email: books@carreg-gwalch.com
website: www.carreg-gwalch.com